Early Childhood Experiences in Language Arts

Early Childhood Experiences in Language Arts

DELMAR PUBLISHERS
COPYRIGHT ©1975
BY LITTON EDUCATIONAL PUBLISHING, INC.

LIBRARY OF CONGRESS CATALOG CARD NUMBER: 74-20265

Printed in the United States of America
Published Simultaneously in Canada by
Delmar Publishers, A Division of
Van Nostrand Reinhold, Ltd.

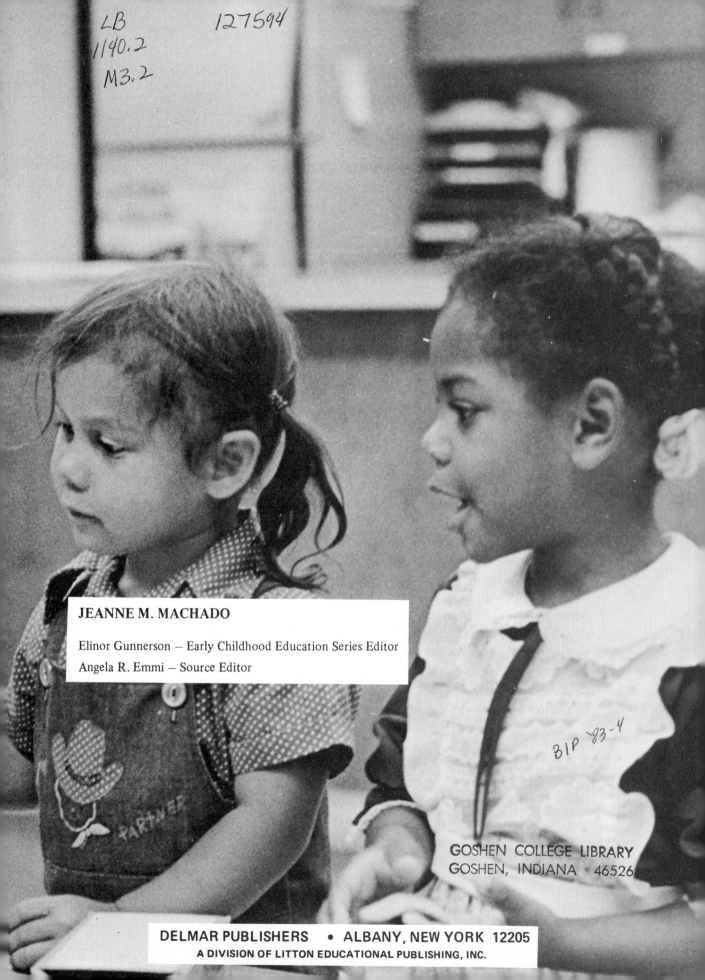

JEANNE M. MACHADO

Elinor Gunnerson — Early Childhood Education Series Editor

Angela R. Emmi — Source Editor

DELMAR PUBLISHERS • ALBANY, NEW YORK 12205
A DIVISION OF LITTON EDUCATIONAL PUBLISHING, INC.

Preface

EARLY CHILDHOOD EXPERIENCES IN LANGUAGE ARTS is intended for college classroom use and as a self-instructional tool. It is hoped that confidence and skill gained by the student will give young children an enthusiastic companion who enjoys and encourages them in their discovery of the language arts.

Teachers who work with young children can make early childhood education centers come alive. Development of skills in the language arts-listening, speaking, writing and reading are all part of an interesting and vital language development program.

The planned experiences and daily activities in this text are based on an understanding of the young child and his potential. The aim of the teacher is to develop the child's comprehension and capacity for use of written and oral language.

Whenever possible the beginning or experienced child care assistant teacher is given practical guides in the planning and presentation of activities. A review of the development of language enables the student to understand individual differences.

The terms child care assistant teacher, child care assistant, child care staff member and teacher are used interchangeably. Teachers are referred to as *she* , and the young child as *he*, for uniformity.

The author, Jeanne M. Machado, received her MA from San Jose State University and attended the University of California at Berkeley. Her experience and professional preparation in the field of childhood education includes teaching in the two-year programs in Child Development as well as personal involvement as the owner of a private preschool center. She has developed commercial materials for use in Early Childhood programs and has designed, furnished and directed developmental programs for children ages two through six years. Ms. Machado is an active participant of several committees which relate to the education of young children and development of their potential.

Other books in the Delmar Early Childhood Education series are:

Creative Activities for Young Children — Mayesky, Neuman and
Wlodkowski

Teaching Young Children — B. Martin

Administration of Schools for Young Children — P. Click

Contents

Section 1 Language Development in the Young Child

unit 1 beginnings of communication

OBJECTIVES

After studying this unit, the student should be able to

- Name factors which influence language development.
- Give examples of early speech characteristics.
- Explain the meaning of perception.

Each child is a special combination of inherited traits and the influence of his environment. The qualities he receives from his parents and the events that occur around him both contribute to his language development.

Development of the ability to communicate begins even before the child is born. The prenatal environment of the child plays an important part in making it possible for the child to express himself and become the person he could be; that is, reach his full potential. Things such as the health of the mother and how it affects the child, the development and health of the unborn child, emotional stress —

all may complicate the child's capability to communicate and learn language.

Language as used in this text refers to a system of communicating ideas or feelings through sounds, signs, marks and gestures. The child learns by using his senses: sight, hearing, smell, taste and touch, figure 1-1. The senses transmit impressions of the things that happen to him. Each *perception* (the act of receiving impressions through the senses) is stored in his mind, serving as a base for future oral and written language, figure 1-2.

Fig. 1-1 The sight and feel of the teddy bear brings a delighted response.

Fig. 1-2 Gathering impressions through the senses.

BEGINNINGS OF COMMUNICATION

Soon after he is born, the child makes his needs known. He cries. Mother responds. She feeds him, holds him, keeps him warm and dry. As the baby grows, he makes another kind of noise; he begins to coo after he is fed. The sound of his mother's footsteps, her voice, her touch, will stop his crying. The baby has related to past experiences. He has learned to connect the senses that are being stimulated with the stored impressions of the past.

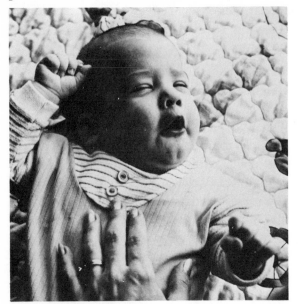

Fig. 1-3 Cooing and touching.

Fig. 1-4 "I can do that."

Babbling is early soundmaking. It begins in infancy and goes on through the toddler age, when the child begins to walk in short, unsteady steps. This is usually the second year of life. Why infants babble is not clear. It is thought that babbling gives the child both the opportunity to use and exercise the mouth, throat and lungs. It also acts as a stimuli to more soundmaking.

As early as three to four months of age, the infant makes more sounds if his mother talks to him and touches him. Touching seems to be important for development as it promotes sound production and the feeling of security, figure 1-3.

By the age of six months, infants show a difference in both the number and kind of sounds they make. The child with warm, loving parents who share a close relationship with each other and the child, responds more readily to the world around him. The child who lacks social and physical contacts is slower in soundmaking; his need for security and love is not being met.

Children imitate early in life. One of the first imitations is social smiling. The protrusion of the tongue follows soon after, figure 1-4. Sound imitation (which begins early in life) progresses to word imitation about the end of the first year.

UNDERSTANDING

At about ten months of age, some infants start to respond to spoken word clues. "Pat-a-cake" may start him clapping and "bye, bye" or "peek-a-boo" bring about other imitations of earlier play activities with his parents.

Often the infant communicates to his parents through many nonverbal actions; one way is by holding up his arms which most often means "I want to be picked up." For other examples see figure 1-5.

Although the infant can now respond to words, he cannot speak the words. Understanding comes first. At this early age there is

Allows food to run out of mouth	Satisfied or not hungry
Pouts	Displeased
Pushes nipple from mouth with tongue	Satisfied or not hungry
Pushes object away	Does not want it
Reaches out for object	Wants to have it handed to him
Reaches out to person	Wants to be picked up
Smacks lips or ejects tongue	Hungry
Smiles and holds out arms	Wants to be picked up
Sneezes excessively	Wet and cold
Squirms and trembles	Cold
Squirms, wiggles, and cries during dressing or bathing	Resents restriction on activities
Turns head from nipple	Satisfied or not hungry

Fig. 1-5 Some common gestures of babyhood.

(From <u>Child Development</u> by Elizabeth B. Hurlock, 1972 – used with permission of McGraw-Hill Company.)

much for him to understand; changes in mother's face, her tone of voice and volume, her actions and gestures, are all things which carry feelings and messages important to his well-being. The understanding of the *tone* in the speech of his parents comes before the understanding of their words, figure 1-6.

WORDS

Repetition of syllables such as *m, d* and *b* in a child's babbling usually happen toward the end of the first year. If "mamma" or "dada" or a close copy is said, parents show attention and joy. Language, especially in the area of speech development, is a two-way process. Reaction is an important feedback to action.

Typically, "no" is said long before "yes." Words are a part of the total situation, and most words have an emotional meaning for the child. For instance the learning of *no,* which to the child usually first means *don't touch.* Later it comes to mean *no, I won't* or *no, I don't want any* but it is still said as "no," the one word.

Words, the child finds, can open many doors. They help him to get things, and cause mother to act in many ways. Vocabulary quickly grows from the names of objects to words which mean action and greetings, such as "hi."

Between eighteen months and four years of age, word use grows at a faster rate of speed than it does in later childhood. Girls usually move slightly ahead of boys in speech ability; this appears to continue through the first grades in school.

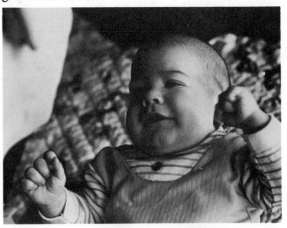

Fig. 1-6 A message of feelings.

CLARITY

Not all of the young child's early speech is clearly understood. A few sounds which give many young children a problem are the *s, th, r,* and *y* sounds. Using words such as *fum* for *some* and *row* for *throw* shows the child's efforts to develop his soundmaking ability. The ability to say all English letter sounds well is normally not reached until age seven or eight. Hearing the difference between sounds, and imitating mouth and tongue positions while controlling airflow is quite a task.

Some early speech is so unclear, it has been called jargon or gibberish. This kind of speech seems to be a long line of syllables with no clear words or meaning; yet it is spoken with expression.

Words are often run together, even in understood speech; the familiar "whatdat?" or "a-gone" are good examples. Single words often stand for complete thoughts, commands, or requests. "Cookie" may mean "I want a cookie" or "Is that a cookie?" Parents guess at meanings with settings and situations giving the clues. They react to what they think the child means. This again points out the two-way process of language development.

EARLY SPEECH

Much of early speech is imitation; but imitation alone cannot explain the child's ability to use language. In addition to the imitations of others, what the child has heard and experienced form an unconscious pattern of speech.

As the young child grows in speaking ability, there is a change in the pattern he has formed. He adds his own words and sentences to his vocabulary and refines them throughout childhood. Slobin has given an interesting example of the way that speech may change from correct usage to incorrect usage.[1]

[1]Dan I. Slobin, Psycholinguistics (Glenview, Ill: Scott, Foresman and Co., 1971)

In all of the cases which have been studied (and these are children of homes where Standard English is spoken, and are usually firstborn children) the first past tenses used are the correct forms of irregular verbs — *came, broke, went,* and so on. Apparently these irregular verbs in the past tense — which are the most frequent past tense forms in adult speech — are learned as separate vocabulary items at a very early age.

Then, as soon as the child learns only one or two regular past tense forms — like *helped* and *walked* — he immediately replaces the correct irregular past tense forms with their incorrect overgeneralizations from the regular forms. Thus children actually say it *came off, it broke,* and *he did it* before they say *it comed off, it breaked,* and *he doed it.* Even though the correct forms may have been practiced for several months, they are driven out of the child's speech by the overregularization, and may not return for years.

Early word phrases and sentences may not always be in correct word order, but key words and tone of voice are present. A child may speak in sentences he has never heard. At first he may omit many words but in time, with good adult models, full sentences will be spoken. Pronouns, adjectives, articles, prepositions and conjunctions appear during the second or third year.

The toddler not only speaks to others, but also to himself and his toys. Talking to himself helps him to store and remember ideas and actions as they occur. Talking to oneself is typical of toddlers and can also be found in children during the preschool period, regardless of age.

By age four or five, adultlike speech patterns should be present in most children. The child moves from simple (one idea) to compound (two ideas) and complex (two or more ideas) sentences in a period of from two to three years.

Sometimes the child creates new words. He invents his own speech when he can't find the right word. Collections of child-created words are quite descriptive. Those who work or live with the young child can generally cite many examples.

CONCEPTS

A *concept* can be defined as the recognition of one or more distinguishing features of a set of objects, persons or events. Concept words are often overused in new situations met by the young child.

The young child who begins to speak early will sometimes use a word from the past and apply it to a new situation. Something in the new situation seems to be similar to a previous one. For a short while, all men are called daddy; also a cow might be seen as a large dog and be called "big goggie." Then, as the child grows he sees small details and differences, figure 1-7. He learns many things from adults and other children; daily activities add to this learning, figure 1-8.

Understanding comes before the ability to speak; many words are used without depth of meaning by young children. Early concepts are not clear because of a child's level of thought. The noted Swiss psychologist and researcher, Jean Piaget, studied the development of children's thinking. He felt that a child goes through a series of six stages in reasoning ability by the time he reaches the age of two years and that language and thought are interrelated.

Maria Montessori, who is well known for her work with young children, also described a sequence of development. Her games and materials are designed to follow an increasing order of difficulty. The step sequence of how a child teaches himself to talk follows.[2]

1. Individual sounds.

2. Syllables.

3. Simple words, often doubled syllables like "dada." This is when the child first is said to speak, because the sound he produces communicates an idea.

[2]Maria Montessori, The Discovery of the Child, translated by M. Joseph Costelloe, (Notre Dame, Indiana: Fides Publishers, 1967)

4. Understanding and saying words that are the names of objects (nouns).

5. Understanding and saying words that refer to qualities of objects named (adjectives).

6. Understanding and saying words that refer to the relationship of objects named.

7. Explosion into language (verbs and the exact form of nouns and adjectives, including prefixes and suffixes.)

8. The forms for present, past, and future tenses of verbs, use of the pronoun as a word that "stands in place of" a name.

9. Construction of sentences with mutually-dependent parts.

Fig. 1-7 "The ball is round. I can play with it."

Fig. 1-8 Living and Learning.

Play with symbols begins during a child's third year. He turns experiences into symbolic action and thought, and words. Before this, the child knew there was a sound (word) for everything in his world. Now he wants to know words and asks "dis?" or "dat?" to whoever will tell him. Soon he will want to know the *why* of things. He will continue to explore, experience, and grow in language ability.

SUMMARY

Each child grows in language ability in his own way. This process starts before birth with the development of sensory organs and continues into childhood. Parents play an important part in the child's growth and mastery of language because his experiences and perceptions come before he learns to speak. Babbling and soundmaking become imitation, and first words appear.

Early speech consists of one or more words put together, sometimes in an unclear manner. Children learn vocabulary quickly and are able to communicate both their thoughts and feelings, especially in warm, secure surroundings.

Language is acquired by the process of receiving and sending messages, with the sensory and motor system dependent on each other.

SUGGESTED ACTIVITIES

- Observe two infants (birth to 12 months). Note situations in which the infants make sounds and how the mothers react to the soundmaking.

- Describe nonverbal communication that you notice or receive in any room with a group of people — classroom, cafeteria, family group, social group — or any other situation where a group of people are assembled.

- Interview mothers with children from 8 to 24 months of age. Ask them to describe their child's ability to get attention and how he communicates what he wants.

- Look up the following words and explain their meanings.
    1. Articulation
    2. Sensory perception
    3. Intonation
    4. Deprivation
    5. Syllables
    6. Speech
    7. Language

REVIEW

A. Place in order of appearance in speech development:
- simple sentences
- babbling
- single words
- adultlike articulation
- run-together words
- compound sentences
- crying
- repeated syllables
- cooing sounds

B. Answer the following questions based on the unit just completed.

1. Name the two basic factors which influence language development.

2. How can parents help the young child to develop language?

3. Name a possible purpose of babbling.

4. Explain why language development is described as a two-way process.

5. Name the sense organs which receive and transmit messages.

6. What is the act of receiving impressions through the senses called?

C. Select the *best* answer.

1. Environment factors which can affect future language development start:

    a. at birth   c. during infancy

    b. before birth   d. during toddlerhood

2. The tone of a mother's voice is

    a. understood when a child learns to speak in sentences.

    b. less important than her words.

    c. understood before actual words are understood.

    d. less important than her actions.

3. Learning to speak is acquired when there is

    a. simple imitation.

    b. a simple, receiving and sending process.

    c. articulation of all English letter sounds.

    d. no connection with other physical factors.

4. According to Montessori, the child is said to speak when he can say a simple word because

    a. articulation begins at that time.

    b. the sound he produces communicates an idea.

    c. he knows what he is saying.

    d. his perceptions are at their highest level at that time.

5. A toddler who talks to toys

    a. is displaying typical behavior.

    b. should be encouraged to talk to people instead.

    c. is considered backward.

    d. should be watched carefully for signs of disturbance.

6. Select the true statements about babbling.

    a. The purpose of babbling is not clearly understood.

    b. Exercises body parts used in speechmaking.

    c. Predicts how early a child will start talking.

    d. Rarely lasts beyond one year of age.

7. Which of the following are true statements?

    a. Early speech is made up of only key words.

    b. Repeated syllables are often first words.

    c. The *s, th, r,* and *y* sounds are difficult for the young child.

    d. New words are rarely created by children.

8. Most children clearly articulate all English speech sounds at

    a. age 4.   c. age 6.

    b. age 5.   d. age 7 or 8.

D. List some ways parents can promote a child's language development.

E. Match the words with the appropriate meaning or example.

1. articulation	a. random sound production
2. babbling	b. mamma, dadda, bye-bye
3. jargon	c. a recognized feature or distinguishing characteristic
4. Jean Piaget	d. reproduction of alphabet letter sounds
5. imitation	
6. vocabulary at 12 months	e. 0-4 words
7. nonverbal communication	f. language and thought are interrelated
8. deprivation	g. "Ibba id amte oogga"
9. repeated syllables	h. repeating sounds and actions
10. concept	i. thumb sucking, smiling, tears
	j. lack of warm, loving care

unit 2 characteristics of preschool language

OBJECTIVES

After studying this unit, the student should be able to

- Describe differences in language of the younger and older preschool child.
- List three reasons why a child care assistant should understand typical language behavior.
- Identify some speech characteristics of the preschooler.

During the preschool years (ages 2-5) a wide range of differences is seen in each child's language ability. Both parents and teachers should accept the temporary limitations because most children will reach adult levels. The main concern of the child care assistant teacher is to serve as a good speech model and to offer the child opportunities and experiences for growth, figure 2-1.

When the speech of a particular child presents a problem, the assistant should talk with other staff members. Investigation is then undertaken. Final decisions about the need for help for a child with speech difficulties are made by parents and qualified professionals in child health and education. Early detection of the cause can increase the chance for quick improvement.

The background of the child care assistant teacher usually includes work experience and study of the young child. The beginnings of language development, sequential steps, and factors which affect self-expression of the child were covered in the preceding unit.

It has been said by many educators, that the child who has *all* the characteristics of a given age group is impossible to find. Most children will possess some speech characteristics which are considered typical for their age level. An idea of what is typical and to be expected of young children is found in this

unit. For the sake of simplicity, early childhood will be divided into the early preschool period, ages 2 and 3 years, and the later preschool period, ages 4 and 5 years.

Fig. 2-1 Exploring together.

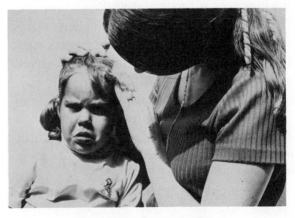

Fig. 2-2 My face says a lot.

THE EARLY PRESCHOOL YEARS

Young children can communicate many needs, desires and feelings, through actions, postures, and facial expressions, figure 2-2. Even when speech is well developed the non-verbal is still present. The raised hand and arm, the fierce clutching of a plaything, or laying "spread eagle" over as many blocks as possible, tells something to both adults and children. The child may also point and pull while saying words. Young children may believe others can read their thoughts because in the child's past, adults anticipated what was needed.

Nonverbal actions may be seen in play — along with squeals, grunts and screams. Often, first conversations are full of these sounds. Frequently used words are possessives, negatives and commands, such as *mine, no,* and *don't.* The volume may be loud, with high-pitched speech. The speech tends to be uneven in rhythm, stopping and starting, rather than flowing like the speech of adults.

Telegram Sentences

The early preschooler omits many words in his sentences. The remaining words remind one of a telegram in which only the essential words are used. These words are key ones and highly informational with the main idea of the message. Without relating them to real life, they may not be understood. Many words found in telegram sentences are nouns; verbs follow as a close second. Some pronouns and adjectives are present with very few, if any, prepositions and connectives. Words may run together and are spoken as single units, such as "whadat?" or "eatem." The order of words in speech may be jumbled as in "outside going me now."

Pronouns are often used incorrectly; *I, me, his, him, her, it, they* and *them* are often confused. Concepts of male, female, living things and other objects may only be partly understood, as shown in the following example.[1]

> "And when a three-year-old says of the ring she cannot find, 'Maybe it's hiding,' the listener wonders if she hasn't yet learned that hiding can be done only by an animate object."

Vocabularies range anywhere from 250 — 1,500 words, showing the high rate of growth which is possible during this period.

Running Commentaries

As a child plays, his actions are sometimes accompanied by a running commentary of what he is doing or what is happening. Talking to himself and talking to another can occur alternately.

Statements directed toward another child do not usually call for answers. They tend to alert the other person to what the talker is doing.

Mention of *egocentric speech* may be found in textbooks on child development. It is defined as speech which does not consider another's point of view. Conversations between young preschoolers may sound like two children talking together about different subjects. Neither child is really listening or reacting to what the other says. When a young child does wish to talk directly to another he may work through an adult. "I want truck." he may say to the adult even if the other child is standing close by.

Repetition

Repetition in speech happens often, sometimes with play and at other times with a purpose in mind. A young child may repeat everything said to him, word for word. Most young preschoolers repeat words or parts of sentences regularly. They quickly imitate a word that catches their fancy; sometimes excitement may be the cause, figure 2-3.

[1] Courtney B. Cazden, <u>Child Language and Education</u>, (New York: Holt, Rinehart and Winston, Inc., 1972)

Free associations and juggling of new words in speech can happen before sleeping periods, but also occurs at other times. It's almost as if having learned a word, it is practiced with pleasure in vocal play.

In conversations, young children may make up words. These created words tend to describe a familiar object, situation or action.

Lack of Clarity

It is felt that about one in every four words of the young preschooler is not understandable. This lack of clarity is caused by inability to control mouth, tongue and breathing muscles and also by the child's listening ability. Typically, articulation of all English speech sounds is not accomplished until age seven or eight, figure 2-4. The young preschooler is only 40%-50% correct in articulation. Young children may omit the sounds at the end of words; "bä" for *ball* is an example. Middle consonants in longer words are also passed over lightly, — "ikeem" for *ice cream,* or "telfone" for *telephone.* Even beginning sounds may be omitted, as in "ellow" for *yellow.*

Substitutions of letter sounds are common. One consonant may take the place of another, until the new sound is mastered; "wabbit" for *rabbit* is a frequent example.

Fig. 2-3 "lookit, lookit, lookit, caterpiller."

Parents sometimes worry about a child who stops, stammers, or stutters. Calling attention and making demands on him can cause tension, making the situation worse instead of better. All children hesitate, repeat, stop and start — it is typical behavior. Searching for the right word takes time; thoughts may come faster than words. Adults need to relax and wait. Speech is a complex sending and receiving process. It takes time. Maintaining patience and optimism is the best course of action.

---

4 years — b, p, m, w, k, g, f, h. If a four-year-old says "ba" for ball, he is within normal speech development limits.

5 years — all the sounds above plus t, d, ng, y. "Dit" for dish is normal. The speech may sound babyish but that is normal.

6 years — all the sounds above plus sh, zh, ch, r, l. If a child says "thither" for "sister" or "tep" for "step," do not worry about his speech for this reason alone.

7 years — all of the sounds above plus s, z, th, j, sl, sk, str, br, pr, tr.

8 years — all letter sounds.

Some speech authorities disagree with expected ages for speech sound emissions, but the above levels are generally accepted.

Fig. 2-4 **Ages at which Children Can be Expected to Correctly make Letter Sounds.** (Todd, V. and Heffernan, H., The Years Before School: Guiding Preschool Children, New York: MacMillan Publishing Co., Inc., 1964)

Young preschoolers become interested in the meaning of new words, and are ready for exposure to a variety of new experiences in the language arts.

THE OLDER PRESCHOOLER

Between 4 and 5 years of age most preschoolers will approach adultlike speech. Their sentences become longer and almost all words are present instead of only key ones.

Their play is active and they copy each other's words. "Monster" or another word swiftly gains interest, and may spread rapidly.

Often self-chatter is still present, and at this age seems to be the child's attempt to relate what is happening with what he already thinks and feels.

Social speech and conversations are now heard and interpreted to a greater degree by others his age. Joint planning of play activities, and active make-believe and role-playing take place, figure 2-5. When playing *mama,* the child acts like one; often teachers or parents see themselves in the role play of the children.

The following recorded observation of four year olds took place at Saint Elizabeth's Day Home, San Jose, California.

Fig. 2-5 Playing together.

IMPACT WORDS

Not all speech used by the older preschooler is appreciated by adults. Name-calling, swearing and offensive words may be used by the active preschooler.

Some words get attention and reaction from both adults and children. The child discovers that sentences as well as words bring about unusual behavior in others. He explores these words and sentences actively, and usually learns what is appropriate and when they can be used. Most of these words

Situation:	Two girls are playing with water.	
	Commentary	**Characteristic**
Debbie:	"Two of those make one of these." (playing with measuring cups.)	Talking to self.
Debbie:	"Two cups or three cups . . . whoops it went over."	Talks about what happened.
Tifine:	"Stop it or else I'll beat you up." (Said to Debbie)	Doesn't respond to another's speech.
Debbie:	"This is heavy." (Holding the 2-cup measuring container full of water.)	Describes perception.
Christine:	"Is it hot?" (Chris just dropped in.)	
Debbie:	"Feel it and see."	Hears another; answers appropriately.
	"It's not hot." (Feeling the water.)	Child talking to self.
Debbie:	"I'm finished not. Oh this is awfully heavy — I'm going to pour it into the bottle.	Talking about what she is doing.

Fig. 2-6 Books capture his attention.

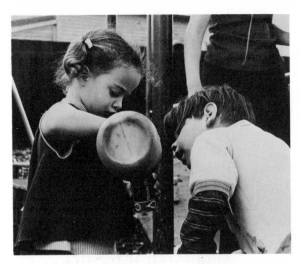

Fig. 2-7 "Want a cup of coffee?"

have *impact value* and if they make people laugh or get him positive reward, they are used over and over.

Many of the words used have a touch of nonsense or silliness; sometimes they rhyme and are fun to say. Often a word rhythm is catchy, and the words are said in a singsong fashion.

To some adults the preschooler might appear loud and wild in speech. His speech seems overly nasal and full of moisture which sprays out in some words. He tends to stand close, and his volume goes up when he is intense about his subject.

He still makes many errors in grammar; in the past tenses of verbs, prepositions, location and time words, to mention a few. His articulation of letter sounds is still growing and about 75% of the English letter sounds are made correctly. Omissions and substitutions of letter sounds still occur.

His vocabulary is usually about 2,000 to 2,500 words. He talks about what he can do and seeks the attention and approval of adults and peers for the things he has done. His questions are many as he not only asks for names, but also the whys and hows of his words.

At this time of early childhood, enjoyment of books, stories and activities with words becomes real for some children. More and more of his time is given to these activities, figure 2-6.

He may still stutter and stop in speech when there is stress or excitement present. The less mature speech of a best friend might be copied, and nonverbal expression is still a part of communication to others.

Most 4 and 5 year olds are avid speakers. They are interested in exploring the real world and also a make-believe one, figure 2-7.

A wide range of individual speech behavior is both normal and possible. Knowing typical behavior helps the child care assistant understand young children. Some younger preschoolers may have the speech characteristics of older preschoolers; older preschoolers may have the speech characteristics of younger ones. Each child comes to the early childhood center as a unique individual, growing in language skill at his own pace.

SUMMARY

Knowing typical and common language development characteristics helps the teacher to understand that children are individual **human beings.**

The speech of the young preschooler (age 2-3) is partly understandable. Child care assistant teachers can use their knowledge in numerous ways, one of which would be alerting staff to the need for special help, and helping parents concerned with their child's speech patterns.

The older child (age 4-5) has an almost adultlike speech. Some behavior and characteristics may be irritating to school staffs and parents, but they indicate physical, mental and social growth. They show positive development in language arts. Exploring both the real and make-believe world with words becomes the child's active pursuit during early childhood years. One does not expect to find each child average and typical when it comes to language development. Individual differences exist and they are treated with acceptance and optimism.

SUGGESTED ACTIVITIES

- Observe a 2, 3, 4 and 5 year old for fifteen-minute periods. Try to write down what is said and a brief description of the setting and actions. Underline typical characteristics described in this unit. Make comparisons between older and younger children.

- Interview two teachers. Ask if any preschool child within their care seems to have special speech or language problems. Write down the teachers' comments and compare them to typical characteristics mentioned in the unit.

- What rules or restrictions concerning the use of inappropriate speech (name-calling, swearing, and screaming) would you expect to find in a preschool center?

- Define: egocentric speech

    running commentary

    omissions

    substitutions

    negatives

    possessives

    consonant

REVIEW

A. Associate the following characteristics with the correct age group. Some may seem to fit both categories; choose the *most* appropriate one. Write the characteristics under the headings: Younger preschooler (2 and 3 years) and Older preschooler (4 and 5 years).

Characteristics of Younger and Older Preschoolers

75% perfect articulation
"Look, I'm jumping."
Telegram sentences
Rhyming and nonsense words
Name-calling and swearing
Repetitions
Substitutions
Omission of letter sounds
Adultlike speech

Nonverbal communication
2,000-2,500 word vocabulary
Talking about what one is doing
Stuttering
Talking through an adult
Role playing
Planning play with others

B. 1. Analyze the following speech observation and list the speech characteristics of each girl.

Situation: Two girls are playing in the housekeeping corner with playhouse equipment. Debbie is setting the table.

Debbie: "Deese daddy's donut. Chugar dem lots. Put chugar on — eatem"

Mary: "The coffee's ready. Ready. Plates goes here. Drink your coffee, daddy. Let's have our coffee. Ouch, it's hot. I burned my troat."

Debbie: "Donut, donut — yum, yummy paghetti, ghetti, pass ghetti. Diss poon, too. Dis ghetti (shows Mary the crumpled paper straws which she has placed on plate.) Me eatem."

Mary: "I need some sauce for the spaghetti. Cupper-pourer can pour on the sauce. Debbie, look at me pour on the sauce. I can eat a whole bunch as much as elfunt."

2. Which girl better fits the characteristics of a young preschooler?

C. Select the correct answers. Many questions have more than one correct response.

1. The younger preschool child (age 2-3 years)

    a. may still grunt and scream in his speech behavior.

    b. always replies to what is said to him by another child.

    c. articulates correctly 75% of the time.

    d. speaks in complete sentences.

2. A truly typical or average child

    a. would have all the characteristics for his age.

    b. is impossible to find.

    c. is one who speaks better than his peers.

    d. sometimes makes up words to fit new situations.

3. Repetition in the speech of the young child

    a. needs careful watching.

    b. is common for children age 2-5.

    c. can be play with words.

    d. happens for a variety of reasons.

4. Name-calling and swearing

    a. may take place during preschool years.

    b. can gain attention.

    c. shows children are testing reactions with words.

    d. only happens with poorly behaved children.

5. A word like blood or ghost

    a. may spread quickly to many children.

    b. has impact value.

    c. can make people listen.

    d. is rarely used in a preschool group.

6. Most younger preschoolers

   a. cannot correctly pronounce all consonants.

   b. omit some letter sounds.

   c. have adultlike speech.

   d. will, when older, reach adult level speech.

7. Stuttering during preschool years

   a. happens often.

   b. should not be drawn to the child's attention.

   c. may happen when a child is excited.

   d. means the child will need professional help to overcome it.

8. "Me wented" is an example of

   a. pronoun difficulty.

   b. a telegram sentence.

   c. verb incorrectness.

   d. the speech of some 2 or 3 year olds.

9. Planning word play with two or more children is found more often in

   a. the 2-3 year old.

   b. the 4-5 year old.

   c. female children.

   d. male children.

10. Knowing typical speech characteristics is important because teachers

    a. must answer the questions of parents.

    b. can help individual children.

    c. interact daily with young children.

    d. should be able to recognize normal behavior.

unit 3 teaching language

OBJECTIVES

After studying this unit, the student should be able to

- List the three roles of a teacher in childhood education.
- Discuss the balances needed in teacher behavior.
- Describe ways a child care assistant can promote language growth.

If an assistant teacher is trying to promote as much growth as she can in the language arts, one should look at the role she plays. She has three main functions in teaching language. First, she serves as a daily *model* of language. How and what she communicates is important. Secondly, she is a *provider* of experiences. Many of these occasions are planned, and others simply happen in the normal course of events. Lastly, the child care assistant teacher is an *interactor,* who gets as much as possible from daily situations, for the growth of the individual child, figure 3-1.

These three functions are kept in balance in light of each child's level and individual needs. The teaching role requires constant decision making. Knowing when to supply or when to withhold information to help self-discovery and knowing when to talk and when to listen are but two important decisions. At the center, the teacher's sensitivity and behavior can make her the child's best ally in the growth of language ability.

MODEL

Teachers not only model speech, but also attitudes and behavior. As children listen to the adults use grammar, intonation, and sentence patterns, they imitate and use the adult as an example.

Adults should use clear, concise speech at a speed and pitch easily understood. Articulation should be as precise as possible.

Complete sentences in Standard English are appropriate. The teacher who adds courtesy words to her speech such as *please* and *thank you* will notice that they become part of the children's speech. The example she sets is one of the strongest features of her teaching, figure 3-2.

The assistant teacher is a model for listening, as well as speaking. Her words will be copied as well as her expressions, pronunciations, and gestures. A quiet teacher tends to have a quiet classroom; an enthusiastic, talkative teacher (who also listens) has a classroom where children talk and share experiences.

The way a child feels about himself will be reflected in his behavior. Teachers may help each child feel that what he says is worth

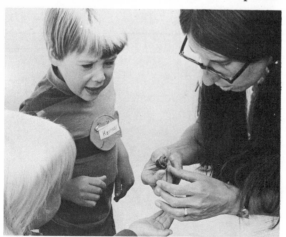

Fig. 3-1 The child care assistant interacts by her words and actions.

Fig. 3-2 Children carefully watch adult examples of speech.

hearing. When children are in surroundings where they feel good about themselves, speaking and listening happen naturally. Therefore, every attempt is made to make the child feel "at home" in school. This is accomplished a number of ways. The child care assistant will find if she accepts each child as a valued human being, unique in his own individual characteristics, the child will learn to accept her also.

Speech is used to solve problems daily and the teacher can build a "together-we-can-work-it-out" feeling. The ways she uses speech to solve differences can help children solve differences verbally instead of with physical aggression.

PROVIDER

Activities planned in language arts cover four broad areas: speaking, listening, written communication, and reading-readiness experiences. Both child care teachers and assistants carry out short- and long-range goals in a step-by-step fashion.

Equipment which helps language growth is found at the preschool center. Recognizing how it can be used is part of providing opportunities for development, figure 3-3.

An early childhood center should be a place where each child both sends and receives

Fig. 3-3 The center should provide the necessary equipment for language development.

language. Teachers are constant senders of words. They go beyond simply trying to help vocabularies grow; they help the child know about the world around him. The use of words is encouraged in both real and make-believe situations.

As a provider of words and activities where words are being used, teachers realize that firsthand experiences promote learning, figure 3-4. The word apple, for instance, becomes real for the child when it is tasted, cut and cooked, picked from a tree, handled and explored in a variety of ways. The child who looks at a picture of an apple while the

Fig. 3-4 "Let me hold it."

teacher tells him about it has limited opportunity. The world is perceived through all the senses. The active preschooler is usually most eager to manipulate and explore what comes his way.

The child, as one of the group, lives words. Teachers often prepare planned activities which give the child a chance to hear ideas and feelings of others. Play with others promotes language growth.

INTERACTOR

An interactor can be defined as a person who is always interested in what a child is saying or doing. She is one who encourages conversation on any subject the child selects. She is someone who is never too busy to talk and share interests and concerns. Time is purposely planned for conversations and, within reason, daily conversation with each child under her care is part of her plan.

Having someone answer with interest rewards the child's speaking. This interest is one type of positive reinforcement. Positive reinforcement can be defined as something good or pleasant that happens to a person after he has performed an activity. Negative reinforcement would be the opposite; either something bad or uncomfortable happens, or nothing happens. Rewarded actions tend to be repeated. The child's speech and listening should be rewarded so that the child will continue to speak and to listen. The rewards most often given by a child care assistant are attention by listening, looking at, smiling, patting, answering, or acting favorably to what a child has said or done.

As the teacher interacts in daily experiences she can help to improve the child's ability to see relationships. Although there is current disagreement as to the teacher's ability to promote *cognitive* growth (the act or process of knowing), she can focus attention and help by both answering and asking questions.

Many times she can help children see clear *links* between already learned and new material. Words are related to the child's mental images which have come through the senses. Language aids memory, and words attached to mental images help the child to retrieve stored information.

As the teacher interacts by supplying words to fit situations, it should be remembered that often a new word needs to be repeated in a subtle manner. It has been said that at least three repetitions of a new word are needed for adults to master it. Young children need more. Teachers often hear the child repeating a new word, as if he is trying to become familiar with it.

A teacher can often help the child focus on something. She can motivate the child's *wanting to know*. Repetition of words and many firsthand activities on the same theme will help the child to form an idea or concept. The child may touch and try something new with the teacher's encouragement.

The reaction of the teacher supplies the child with feedback to his actions. The teacher is responsible for reinforcing the use of a new word and ensuring that the child has a good attitude about himself as a speaker.

Daily she can take advantage of unplanned things that happen to promote language and speech. Catherine Landreth provides an illustration:

While children were sitting in a story group, John noticed a mobile, hung from the ceiling above, was spinning. "Look," said John pointing, "it's moving!" "How come?" said another child. "Someone must have touched it," said Mary. "Stand up, Mary and see if you can touch it," added the teacher, standing up and reaching herself. "I can't reach it either." "Maybe it spins itself," contributed Bill. "No, it can't spin itself," said another child. "Let's see," said the teacher. She got a piece of yarn with a bead tied to the end and held it out in front of the children. It was still. Then she held it near the mobile, which was in a draft of a window. The string swayed gently. "The window, the window is open," suggested the children. "Yes, wind is coming through the window," said John. "And making it move," said all the children, pleased with their discovery. The teacher held the string so the children could blow at it. "Look, I'm the wind," said one of them. That afternoon, outside, the children were given crepe paper streamers to explore wind direction. They were also read <u>Gilberto and the Wind</u>, which tells what happens when wind blows the sail of a boat, the arm of a windmill, the smoke from the chimney, and a child's hat and hair.[1]

To make the most of the unforeseen is a valuable skill. Being alert to the interest of the child is the key. Moving into a situation with skill and trying to help the child find and tell what he has found is part of promoting word growth.

Teachers need a clear understanding of how children learn words and concepts. The following chart includes guidelines for teachers' actions to accompany the child's progress toward new learning. Specific examples are shown on page 22.

Language Learning and Teacher Interaction	
Child Activity	**Teacher Actions**
• Focuses on an object or activity	• Name the object, or offer a statement describing the actions or situation. (Supplies words)
• Manipulates and explores the object or situation using touch, taste, smell, sight, sound organs.	• Try to help child connect this object or action to child's past experience through simple conversation. (Builds bridge between old and new)
• Fits this into what he already knows. Develops some understanding.	• Help the child see details through simple statements or questions. (Focusing on identifying characteristics)
	• Ask "Show me . . ." or "Give me . . ." questions which ask for a nonverbal response. (Prompting)
	• Put child's action into words. (Example: "John touched the red ball.") (Modeling)
	• Ask the child for a verbal response. "What is this called?" "What happened when . . .?" (Prompting)
• Uses a new word or sentence which names, describes, classifies or generalizes a feature or whole part of the object or action.	• Give a response in words indicating the truth factor of the response. "Yes, that's a red ball." or "It has four legs like a horse, but it's called a cow." (Corrective or reinforcing response)
	• Extend one word answers to full simple sentence if needed. (Modeling)
	• Suggest an exploration of another feature of the object or situation. (Extending interest)
	• Ask a memory or review question. "Tell me about . . ." (Reinforcing and assessing)

[1]Catherine Landreth, <u>Preschool Learning and Teaching,</u> (New York: Harper and Row, 1972)

I. (Child with flower)

Child: "Pretty."

Teacher: "Yes, you have a pretty flower."

Child: "Pretty flower."

Teacher: "Sally's touching the pretty flower."

Child: "Me touching flower."

Teacher: "Smell the flower." (Holding it to her nose.)

Child: "Mm." (Child smells.)

Teacher: "The pretty flower smells good. What's this called?"

Child: "Pretty flower."

Teacher: "Yes, it's a pretty flower. Does it smell good?"

Child: "Pretty flower smells good."

Teacher: "Touch the stem." (Shows with hands.)

II. (Child with cookie)

Child: "Look teacher, cookie."

Teacher: "Oh, you have a . . . .?"

Child: "Cookie."

Teacher: "Are you going to eat the cookie?"

Child: "I'm going to bite it."

III. (Child on swing)

Teacher: "Hold on tightly, Nicki."

Child: "Why?"

Teacher: "If you don't, you might slip off the seat."

Child: "Why?"

Teacher: "Because I'm going to push you now. You asked me to make you go higher. If I push you hard, you might slip off the seat."

Child: "I like to go higher."

Teacher: "Okay, hold on tightly, and I'll push you."(Pushes) "Are you going high?"

BALANCE

In all of her roles the assistant needs to maintain a balance. The child care assistant teacher should try to

- give, but withhold when self-discovery is practical and possible.
- interact, but not interfere or dominate the child's train of thought or action.
- give support, but not hover constantly.
- talk, but not overtalk.
- listen, but not remain silent.
- provide times for the child to speak, figure 3-5.

Part of the balance the teacher seeks will be her attempt to be a model, a provider, and an interactor who best suits the ability of each child. As a model, her example offers the child a next step; a little above, but not too far above, what the child is able to do already. In doing this the child care assistant watches and listens as she works with individual children, learning as much from the misunderstandings or mistakes as she does from those behaviors, words and actions she feels are correct and appropriate. This does not mean her motive is always to teach, for the teacher also enjoys living and communicating with the children. It does mean that she is ready to make the most of every situation as they enjoy school together.

A child care assistant's attitude toward child growth in language should be one of optimism, that is, provide the best she can while realizing the child will grow and learn language skill when he is ready. Early childhood centers plan for as much growth as possible in language abilities with teachers who model, provide and interact during activities.

SUMMARY

Teachers function as models, providers of opportunities for language growth, and

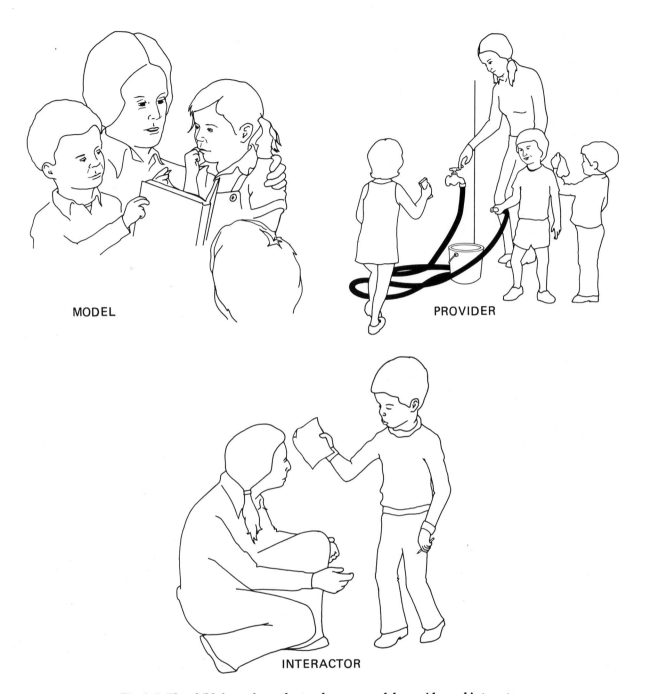

MODEL

PROVIDER

INTERACTOR

Fig. 3-5 The child depends on the teacher as a model, provider and interactor.

interactors. Children copy many behaviors and attitudes of both adults and peers.

Words are symbols for objects, ideas, actions, and situations. The child care assistant teacher can promote the learning of new words and help the child to recognize links between past and present.

A delicate balance exists. Sensitive decisions are often made to maintain an atmosphere which affords each child maximum growth opportunities. Rewarding a child's actions tends to make those actions happen again. Examples of teacher behavior to promote early childhood language development are:

Models	Provides	Interacts
speech	opportunities	focusing attention
intonation	activities	asking questions
pitch	equipment	motivating
articulation	materials	planning repetitions
attitudes	words	giving feedback
actions	information	reinforcing
grammar	the necessity to speak	taking advantage of
sentence patterns	group situations	unplanned events
Standard English	listening	listening
courtesy words		
listening		
pronunciation		
enthusiasm		
care and concern		
problem solving		

SUGGESTED ACTIVITIES

- Observe a teacher interacting with a preschool child. Note the teacher's speech and actions which make the child feel that what he (the child) says is important.

- Describe three typical preschool situations that would make it necessary for a child to speak.

- Listen intently to three adults (take notes). How would you evaluate them as speech models — good, average, poor. State the reasons for your decision.

- Describe what is meant by the following terms.

Standard English	Image
Symbol	Cognitive
Example	Positive reinforcement
Motivation	Interactor

REVIEW

A. Name the three basic functions of the early childhood teacher.

B. List five examples of each of the aforementioned functions.

C. Following is an observation of an assistant teacher and children. Read it through. Then indicate what you feel was appropriate behavior and inappropriate behavior on the part of the assistant teacher in the light of language development.

Situation: Teacher is conducting a sharing time with Joey, Mabel, Maria and Chris.

Teacher: "It's time for sharing, please sit down children."

Joey: "I want to share first!"

Teacher: "You'll have your turn, you must learn to wait."

Mabel: "I can't see."

Teacher: "Yes you can."
"Maria, you're sitting quietly and not talking. You may go first."

Maria: "This is a book about Mickey. Mickey clips."

Joey: "What's clips, teacher?"

Teacher: "You're next, Joey."

Joey: "Mickey on T.V. teacher. Tomorrow I went to the fire station. The fireman let me wear his badge, like this."

Chris: "Fireman's truck red. Goes whee – whee."

Teacher: "It's Joey's turn, Chris, would you wait to talk?"

Mabel: "I want to go, now!"

Teacher: "Mabel, you must have your turn to share before you can go."

Mabel: "I see a butterfly on the window."

Teacher: "Later, Mabel, you can go outside later."

D. What two factors should be considered by the assistant teacher in her goal to keep her main functions in balance?

E. The following multiple-choice questions require more than one correct response. Select the appropriate items.

1. The child care assistant is a model for

   a. speech.

   b. attitudes.

   c. speech more often than parents may be.

   d. speech only during planned activities.

2. It is more important for the young child

    a. to like to speak than have him speak correctly.

    b. to participate than to sit quietly.

    c. to speak than to listen.

    d. to have the teacher tell him about something than to have him explore it himself.

3. Assistants reinforce learning by

    a. using speech to solve problems.

    b. praising the child's use of a new word.

    c. motivating the child's "wanting to know."

    d. linking the old with the new ideas.

4. When the assistant speaks

    a. she should attempt to use correct articulation.

    b. she should speak in full sentences.

    c. she should make sure each child responds by speaking.

    d. she should refrain from "overtalking."

5. Preschool children

    a. are also speech models.

    b. rarely teach each other new words.

    c. play and use words in play.

    d. have growing vocabularies only when teachers act appropriately.

6. Words are

    a. symbols for real happenings.

    b. related to stored images.

    c. learned through the senses.

    d. not labels for concepts.

Section 2 Listening — A Language Art

unit 4 developing listening skills

OBJECTIVES

After studying this unit the student should be able to

- List five levels of listening.
- Discuss teaching techniques which promote good listening habits.
- Demonstrate how to plan an activity which promotes auditory perception.

Auditory perception refers to the process of being aware of sounds and their meanings. At birth, the world with its multitude of sounds bombard the baby. From this mass of confusion, certain sounds become familiar and take on meanings. No one formally teaches an infant to listen, understand and discriminate.

Many children develop the ability to listen carefully to the speech of others during early childhood; others do not. Since language growth has been described as a receiving process followed by a sending process, a child's listening ability is extremely important. This ability to listen must come before the child can learn to speak.

Most early childhood centers contain many opportunities to listen. Teacher-planned or child-created play has sounds associated with it. A quality program sharpens a child's listening, and offers a variety of types of experiences. Listening is not left to chance; planned programs develop skills, figure 4-1.

LISTENING LEVELS

Listening is *multifarious,* that is, learning may occur in a variety of ways. A person does not always listen for knowledge, but may listen to a sound because it is pleasing to the ear. The first time a child discovers the sound made by pots and pans, he is fascinated. Preschoolers often make their own pleasurable or rhythmic sounds with whatever is available.

The human voice can be interesting, threatening or monotonous to individual children depending on past experience. Silence also carries its individual meaning. Many teachers have had the experience of believing a child had a hearing problem, only to find that he was inattentive for other reasons.

A child may listen yet not understand. He can miss sound differences, or listen without evaluating what he hears. This indicates that listening involves a variety of skills and

Fig. 4-1 Early childhood centers are full of opportunities to listen.

levels. In order to provide growing opportunities, child care assistants should be aware of various listening abilities. Different listening levels are shown at the bottom of the page.

The goal of a good program in early childhood language arts is to guide the young child toward development of these levels.

TEACHER SKILLS

Good listening habits are important in school situations. Instructions from teachers should be clear and simple with a sequence of what comes first, next, and last; usually instructions need not be repeated when given clearly and simply. Often when the attention of the group is required, a signal is used. The ringing of a small bell, playing a piano chord, or a flick of the lights means it's time to listen, figure 4-2. The silent pause before beginning an activity can be used effectively to focus attention on listening.

Often teachers use a short song, or fingerplay, or body movement activity, to stimulate interest and draw the group together. This helps children focus on what is to follow.

Praise and smiles can reward listening. Positive, specific statements such as, "Michael, I liked the way you listened to what Tommy had to say, before you started talking." or, "Thank you, Berti for waiting so quietly. Now we can all hear the beginning of the story.", give children feedback on expected listening behavior.

Fig. 4-2   A child signals it's time for a snack.

Appreciative listening. The child finds pleasure and entertainment in hearing music, poems and stories. It is best to begin with this type of listening because it is passive, but personal for each child.

Purposeful listening. The child follows directions, and gives back responses.

Discriminative listening. The child becomes aware of changes in pitch and loudness. He differentiates sounds in the environment. Eventually, he is able to discriminate the speech sounds.

Creative listening. The child's imagination and emotions are stimulated by his listening experiences. He expresses his thoughts spontaneously and freely through words, or actions, or both.

Critical listening. The child understands, evaluates, makes decisions, and formulates opinions. To encourage this critical listening, the teacher may pose such questions as: "What happens when we all talk at once?" "What if everyone wanted to play in the playhouse at the same time?" The child must think through the responses, decide the most logical solution to the problem, and present a point of view.

From Louise B. Scott, <u>Learning Time With Language Experiences</u> (New York: McGraw-Hill Book Co.)

Rewarded behavior is usually repeated and becomes a habit. Child care assistants should consistently notice correct listening behavior, and comment favorably about it to the children.

AUDITORY PERCEPTION

Ears respond to sound waves. These sounds go to the brain and become organized in relation to past experience. The same process is used in early childhood and later when the child learns to read. His development in language depends upon the auditory process.

Educational activities which give practice and help perfect auditory skills usually deal with the following objectives.

- Sustaining attention span
- Following directions or commands
- Imitating sounds
- Identifying and associating sounds
- Using auditory memory
- Discriminating between sounds (tempo, pitch, intensity)

The *intensity* of a sound refers to its degree of force, strength, energy. *Pitch* refers to the highness or lowness of sound. *Tempo* refers to the rate of speed of a musical piece or passage; in other words, the rate of motion or activity.

SETTINGS FOR LISTENING

When preparing listening activities, the assistant teacher plans for success. Activities take place in room areas with a minimum of distracting sound and visual stimuli. Screens, dividers, and bookcases are helpful, figure 4-3. Heating and lighting are checked and comfortable seating is provided. Decisions concerning the size of a group are important. In general, the younger the group, the smaller it should be, and the shorter the length of the lesson.

Fig. 4-3 Placement of a piece of furniture or cabinet can reduce distractions.

Since listening cannot be forced, the key is to motivate, figure 4-4. Some schools offer children the choice of joining a group listening activity or playing quietly nearby. Teachers find that an interesting experience attracts children who are nearby. When activities are enjoyable and successful, the child who was hesitant may look forward to new experiences. A teacher can "turn on" or "turn off". She knows when the children are "with her," and can end, change or modify when necessary. Careful watching for feedback is part of developing active listening by the child. We have all had teachers who did not know when to stop, and we have all had teachers to whom we listened eagerly. One of the skills of the successful teacher is to complete the learning

Fig. 4-4 The child care assistant sits with a child and encourages him to listen.

activity before the class becomes restless. The capacity of the active preschooler to remain seated for any length of time is something every assistant teacher must face. It must be considered of particular importance especially when listening is necessary to the activity.

SUMMARY

The ability to listen matures with experience and exposure. Young children vary in their ability to listen. Listening ability can be divided into a series of levels — appreciative, purposeful, discriminative, creative and critical.

Proper use of planned activities, teacher interaction, and equipment can bring about opportunities to develop the child's auditory perception skills.

Listening cannot be forced, but is motivated. Signals and positive reinforcement can help to form habits. Settings which limit stimuli and control the size of groups are desirable. When teachers are watchful and act when restlessness or lack of interest develop during planned activities, listening remains active. One of the responsibilities of the child care assistant is to plan carefully so that young children consistently want to hear what is being offered.

SUGGESTED ACTIVITIES

- With a small group of classmates, discuss some of the ways a home or school environment can make young children "tune out."

- Watch a listening activity in a preschool center. Then answer the following questions:

  - How did the teacher prepare the children for listening?

  - What elements of the activity captured interest?

  - How was child interest held?

  - Did the teacher have an opportunity to praise listening?

  - Did children's behavior during the activity seem important to the teacher?

  - Was this the kind of activity that should be repeated? If so, why?

- Observe preschoolers in group play. Write down any examples of appreciative, purposeful, discriminative, creative or critical listening.

- Plan a listening activity. Describe the materials you will need, how the activity will start, what is to happen during the activity, and state what auditory perception skills you included in your plan.

- In a paragraph, describe the difference between motivating a child to listen and forcing a child to listen.

REVIEW

A. Five levels of listening have been discussed. After each of the following statements, identify the listening level which best fits the situation.

1. After hearing an indian drum on a record, Brett slaps out a rhythm of his own on his thighs while dancing around the room.

2. During the story of The Three Little Pigs , Mickey pops out with "He's not berry nice!" in reference to the wolf's behavior in the story.

3. Kimmie is following Chris around. Chris is repeating "Swishy, fishy-co-co-pop," over and over again, both giggle periodically.

4. Debbie tells you about the little voice that small Billy Goat Gruff has and the big voice that big Billy Goat Gruff has in the story of the Three Billy Goats Gruff.

5. Peter has asked if he can leave his block tower standing during snacktime instead of putting the blocks away, as you have requested, because he wishes to return and build it higher. He then listens for your answer.

B. Name the objectives which are used in planning listening activities.

C. Select the correct answers. All have more than one correct reply.

1. Most parents unconsciously teach preschoolers

    a. to develop auditory perception.

    b. attitudes toward listening.

    c. to listen to their teachers.

    d. many words.

2. A teacher can promote listening by

    a. demanding a listening attitude.

    b. use of a signal to listen.

    c. use of praise.

    d. telling a child he is not listening.

3. Critical listening happens when

    a. the child relates what is new to past experience.

    b. the child disagrees with another statement.

    c. the child makes a comment about a word being good or bad.

    d. teachers plan thought-provoking questions, and the child has the maturity he needs to answer them.

4. Children come to early childhood centers with

    a. individual variation in ability to listen.

    b. habits of listening.

    c. all the abilities and experiences needed to be successful in planned activities.

    d. a desire to listen to anyone and everyone.

5. A child's ability to follow a series of commands depends

    a. on his auditory memory.

    b. on how clearly the commands were stated.

    c. on how well his ears transmitted the sounds to his brain, and how well the brain sorted the information.

    d. on how well he can imitate the words of the commands.

6. What is the meaning of the statement "Listening is multifarious."?

7. Explain what is meant by *intensity, pitch* and *tempo.*

unit 5 listening activities

OBJECTIVES

After studying this unit the student should be able to

- Describe three listening activities, stating what auditory perception skill is promoted in each.
- Plan and present a listening activity.
- State two ways tape recorders and records can be used for listening activities.

Listening activities are used to increase enjoyment, vocabulary and attention span. In this unit, the activities focus on the development of auditory skills through verbal listening and responding interactions. Activities which further develop these skills through the use of books and stories are found in later units.

"CAN YOU SAY IT LIKE I DO?"

Objective

Imitating sounds.

Materials

None

Introduction and Activity

The teacher says, "Can you change your voice like I can?"

"My name is _____ ."	(softly whispering)
Teacher's Name	
,, ,, ,,	(loudly)
,, ,, ,,	(low voice)
,, ,, ,,	(high voice)
,, ,, ,,	(fast)
,, ,, ,,	(slowly)
,, ,, ,,	(with mouth held closed)
,, ,, ,,	(with mouth held open)
,, ,, ,,	(holding nose)

The teacher selects a child who talks easily.

"Now let's see if we can change our voice, like Billy. Try it in a whisper, Billy. Do it any way you want, Billy."

The teacher gives others a chance who wish to perform. This activity may be followed up with a body-action play with voice changes.

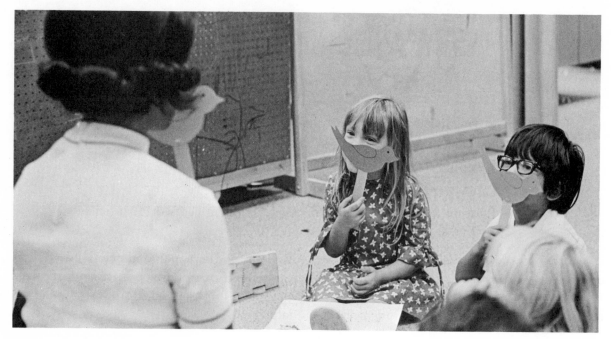

Fig. 5-1 Parakeet talk.

PARAKEET TALK

Objective

To imitate sounds.

Materials

Popsicle sticks and colored construction paper. Cut out parakeets from colored construction paper and paste them on popsicle sticks. All forms can be traced and cut from one pattern, figure 5-1.

Introduction and Activity

Discuss birds who imitate what people say. Distribute parakeet forms. Begin with something like "We can pretend to be parakeets too."

Teacher:	Hi parakeets!
Children:	Hi parakeets!
Teacher:	Pretty bird.
Children:	Pretty bird.
Teacher:	Now let's hear from Julie, the yellow parakeet. Can the blue parakeet (Mike) say whatever the green parakeet (Sue) says? Let's see.

This activity leads well into a record with children pretending to be birds flying.

Suggest that the children flap their wings through a door to an outdoor area, or take a walk to listen for bird sounds.

Fig. 5-2 "If you hear a mistake, raise your hand."

"LISTEN, OOPS A MISTAKE!"

Objective

To associate and discriminate word sounds with objects.

Materials

Four or five common school objects (pencil, crayon, block, toy, cup, doll, etc.). A low table.

Introduction and Activity

Talk about calling things by the wrong name. Then name the objects on the table. Begin with something like, "Have you ever called your friend by the wrong name?"

> Teacher: When you call your friend by the wrong name you've made a mistake. Look at the things here on the table. I am going to name each of them (she names them correctly). All right, now see if you can hear my mistakes. This time I'm going to point to them too. If you hear a mistake, raise your hand and say, "oops, a mistake!" Let's say that together once, "oops, a mistake!" Good. Are you ready? Listen: crayon, ball, doll, cup.

Change objects and give a child a chance to make a mistake while the others listen, figure 5-2.

This activity can later be followed with the story of *Moptop* (by Don Freeman, Children's Press) in which a long-haired red-headed boy is mistaken for a mop.

ERRAND GAME

Objective

To follow verbal commands.

Materials

None.

Introduction and Activity

Start a discussion about doing things for mother. Include getting objects from other rooms, neighbors, etc. Tell the children you are going to play a game in which each person looks for something another has asked for.

> Teacher: "Get me a book, please."
> "Can you find me a leaf, please."

Items to ask for may include a rock, blade of grass, piece of paper, block, doll, crayon, toy car, sweater, hat, clothes hanger, blanket, etc. Send children off one at a time. As they return, talk to each about where they found their item. While the group waits for all members to return, the teacher's assistant can name all the returned items, put them in a row, ask children to cover their eyes while one is hidden, and then ask the children to guess which item was removed.

If interest is still high, the assistant can again give the command that the items be returned, and repeat the game by sending the children for new items.

JACK-IN-THE-BOX

Objective

To discriminate sounds by listening for a signal, and responding to it.

Materials

None. (To increase fun, cardboard boxes may be used. Tops should open easily. Be sure that the child is not afraid to climb inside the box).

Introduction and Activity

Recite the following rhyme in a whispered voice until the word "pop" is reached. Using hand motions, hide thumb in fist and let it pop up on the word "pop" each time it is said.

> Jack-in-the Box, Jack-in-the-Box, where can you be?
> Hiding inside where I can't see?
> If you jump up, you won't scare me.
> Pop!, Pop!, Pop!

Suggest children squat and pretend to be jack-in-the-boxes. Ask them to listen and jump up only when they hear the word "pop."

Try a second verse if the group seems willing.

> Jack-in-the-Box, Jack-in-the-Box, you like to play,
> Down in the box you won't stay.
> There's only one word I have to say,
> Pop!, Pop!, Pop!

PIN ON SOUND CARDS (ANIMALS AND BIRDS)

Objective

To associate and imitate sounds, and to use auditory memory.

Materials

Safety pins or masking tape, File cards (3 x 5) with pictures of birds and animals (gummed stickers of animals and birds are available in stationery stores and from supply houses). Suggestions: duck, rooster, chick (peep-peep), owl, goose (honk-honk), woodpecker (peck-peck), horse, cow, cat, dog, sheep, lion, mouse, turkey, bee, frog, donkey, seal (clap-clap).

Introduction and Activity

Have a card pinned on your shirt or blouse before the children enter the room. This will start questions. Talk about the sound your card makes.

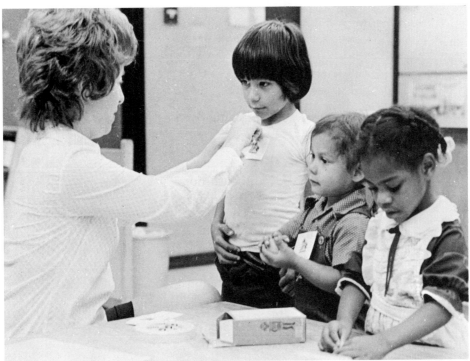

Fig. 5-3 Pinning on Sound Cards.

Practice it with the children. Ask who would like a card of his own. Have the children come, one at a time, while you pin on the cards. Talk about the animal and the sound it makes. Imitate each sound with the group. Play a game where one of the children makes an animal noise and the child with the right card stands up and says,

"That's me, I'm a _____ ."

name of animal

Children usually like to wear the cards the rest of the day and take them home if possible, figure 5-3.

GUESS WHAT?

Objective

To identify and discriminate common sounds.

Materials

A bell, hand eggbeater, paper bag to crumple, baby rattle, tambourine, drum, stapler, any other noisemaker. A room divider, screen, table turned on its side, or blanket taped across a doorway.

Introduction and Activity

Ask children to guess what you have behind the screen.

Teacher: "Listen, what makes that sound?"

(With younger children it's best to introduce each item with its name first). Ask a child to come behind the screen and make the next noise, figure 5-4.

Fig. 5-4 "Guess what!"

Variation

- Clap simple rhythms behind the screen and have children imitate them. Rhythms can be made up by using full claps of the hands with light claps and pauses at regular intervals; for example, a loud clap followed by two light ones and a pause repeated over and over.

- Ask a child to sit in the "guessing chair" with his back to the group. From the group, select a child to say "Guess my name." If the first child answers correctly, he gets a chance to select the next child who is to sit in the guessing chair.

PLAY TELEPHONES

Objective

To focus on listening and responding.

Materials

Paper, blunt toothpicks, string, two small tin cans with both ends removed (check for rough edges).

Introduction and Activity

Cover one end of each tin can with paper. Make a small hole, insert long string in hole, tie string around blunt toothpicks. (Paper cups can be substituted for the tin cans.) Make enough sets for the group. Demonstrate how they work.

"WHO DIDN'T SPEAK?"

Objective

To identify and associate voices.

Materials

Cassette tape recorder (headset plug-in, optional), cassette tape, snapshot or Polaroid pictures of the children, cardboard, clear contact paper, scissors, a small box to store pictures and cassette tape.

Introduction and Activity

Record children's voices one at a time on the tape. It is best to have the children prepared with a short rhyme or song they know — or to have a collection of objects or pictures — that they can tell you about. In random order, line up all the pictures of the children whose voices are on the tape. As each child speaks, pick up his picture and put it aside. (Most will talk about themselves in the snapshots and what they're doing.) When the tape is finished, point to the remaining pictures.

      Teacher: "Whose voice didn't we hear?"

Have a child name the children in the remaining pictures. Mix pictures together again, adding others whose voices are not on the tape, and take away some of those who did not speak in the first game. Try again if children are interested and the group is fairly small. Fatigue and inattention result if the activity is repeated when the children have been at it too long.

RECORDS

The use of equipment in activities to promote listening skills is common. Some schools have listening centers with headset plug-ins. Under supervision, children may operate the equipment themselves.

Records for auditory perception are made by some companies who specialize in children's records. Most records actively move the child to listen for a signal, to listen to directions, or to listen to sounds. Some include body movements along with listening skills.

Not all records manufactured are of clear quality, or contain appropriate subject matter for young children. Before using a record with children, a child care assistant teacher should first listen to the record herself. The following criteria may be used to judge a record's worth:

- Is the subject matter appropriate?
- Is it clearly presented?
- Is it interesting to the young child?
- Does it meet the teaching objective?

Many records have been made of children's classics. Activities designed to improve listening skills are also available on records. These will be discussed later.

TAPE RECORDERS

Tape recorders can both fascinate and frighten children. Assistant teachers find them valuable tools for listening activities. Under the teacher's supervision, children can explore and enjoy sounds. Unfortunately, most tape recorders are delicate, requiring the teacher to operate them and supervise their use.

LANGUAGE MASTER

A language master is a sturdy, portable piece of equipment. It can both record and play back instantly. Cards are inserted in a left-to-right fashion. Although a child needs supervision in its use, he can learn how to use it in a short time.

This machine has many listening-activity possibilities, and schools find it a valuable piece of equipment.

SUGGESTED ACTIVITIES

- Choose one of the activities found in the suggested resource list in the Appendix, p. 161. Present the activity to a group of preschoolers. Then answer the following questions.

  Was the activity interesting to the children? Were they able to perform the auditory perception tasks? Would you change the activity in any way if you presented it again?

- Find or create five additional listening activities. After source, state the title of the book where you found the activity idea. If the idea is original, indicate by using the word "self." Use a tape recorder in one activity.

  Source   Materials Needed

  Name of Activity   Description of Activity

  Objective

- Records are used for activities in auditory perception and also for the development of listening skills. List three records that you feel could be used for this purpose. Bring one of the records to the class at the next meeting. Be ready to demonstrate its use. Include the following information about each record.

  Name of record.

  Manufacturer's name and address.

  Price.

  Briefly describe content of record.

  Name the listening skill involved.

- Select a popular children's television program to watch. Study the following questions prior to watching. Answer them after viewing the program.

  Name, time, date of viewing.

  Were there attempts to build listening skills? If so, what were they?

  In what ways would the program interest preschoolers?

  Do you have any criticism of the program?

  Could teachers of early childhood education use any techniques seen in their auditory perception activities?

REVIEW

1. In what ways do children's records affect listening and movement?

2. List the criteria for record selection.

unit 6 reading to children

OBJECTIVES

After studying this unit, the student should be able to

- State three goals for reading books to young children.
- Describe the criteria for book selection.
- Demonstrate suggested techniques for reading a book to a group of children.

Books provide an excellent source for listening activities for the young child. Seeing, touching and interacting with books should be part of a quality program in early childhood education.

A child care assistant needs to understand that books play an important part in language development. When staff members have goals clearly defined and kept in mind, a much better job is done. Goals are defined as the ends towards which effort is directed; in other words, what the school is trying to accomplish.

Many children have been read to at home; others have not. A teacher may have the joy of offering the child his first contact with stories and books, figure 6-1.

GOALS

Children can gain much from books. The first goal should be to provide enjoyment.

The feeling that books are interesting, can hold new experiences and can be enjoyed alone or with others, is of utmost importance. The child's attitude toward books, and how competent he feels when he is in a book-reading situation is of prime concern. One can teach a child to read and make it such an unpleasant experience that he avoids reading books. In contrast, some children enjoy a lifetime of reading.

Not every child in preschool is interested in books or sees them as something to enjoy. It is the teacher's responsibility to encourage the child's interest in books, figure 6-2. There is no such thing as forcing a child to like books; that is a decision he makes for himself based on his own experiences. Part of the positive feeling toward books depends on whether the child feels successful and competent during bookreading time. This depends on

Fig. 6-1 Mixed reactions to a story.

Fig. 6-2 Teacher encourages book exploration.

how skillfully the child care assistant acts and reacts, and how well the sessions are planned.

A second goal of reading books to children is the *presentation of knowledge.* Books can acquaint the child with new words, ideas, facts, and experiences. These are given in a different form than spoken conversation. In books, sentences are complete; in conversation they may not be. Stories and illustrations follow a logical sequence.

Assistant teachers promote the fact that books can be used as resources. When one wants to find out about things, picture dictionaries, books on special subjects such as animals, birds, fish, child encyclopedias and similar books are used to find out facts. Teachers, when asked questions, often use books as the source for answers. When the child care assistant says, "I don't know, but I know where I can find out," she demonstrates that books are used for finding answers. She tells where she is going to look and follows through by showing the child where it is found.

The third goal deals with the *development of skills.* Attention can become focused, and some educators feel attention span can be increased during listening times. Different levels of listening such as discriminative, appreciative, purposeful, creative and critical can all be present in one book.

Children learn how to care for books, where and how they can be used. Attitudes about books as personal possessions begin in early childhood.

SELECTION

The teacher is responsible for selecting books which meet the stated goals. Some books may fill the needs completely; others only partially meet the goals. Often staff members are asked to choose new books to buy. The local library offers the opportunity to borrow books which help to keep story-telling time fresh and interesting.

A book that one child is especially fond of may not be popular with another. The teacher will find that some stories appeal more to one group than another. Old favorites are usually enjoyed. There is a security, a feeling of being "at home," a oneness with the group, when the teacher reads an old favorite. The child looks forward to a familiar part or event in the story.

CRITERIA

Following are a series of questions a child care assistant should ask when selecting a child's book.

1. Could I read this book *enthusiastically* showing enjoyment of the story?

2. Are the contents of the book *appropriate* for the children with whom I work?

   a. Can the children relate some parts to their lives and past experience?
   Some books have subjects beyond their interest, ability or experience.

   b. Can the children identify with one or more of the characters?
   Look at children's classics and Mother Goose. Almost all of the stories have a well-defined character with which children have something in common. Teachers find different children identify with different characters, the wolf instead of one of the pigs in "The Three Little Pigs," for example.

   c. Does the book have directly quoted conversation?
   If it does this can add interest; for example, "Are you my mother?" he said to the cow.

   d. Will the child benefit by attitudes and models found in the book?
   Violence and frightening events are part of some fairy tales. Racial inferences may appear in other stories.

3. Was the book written with an understanding of *preschool age level* characteristics?

   a. Is the text too long to sit through? Are there too many words?

   b. Are there enough colorful illustrations or pictures to hold attention? If not, is the story good enough to hold interest without them, figure 6-3.

   c. Is the size of the book suitable for easy handling in groups or for individual viewing?

   d. Can the child participate in the story by speaking or making actions? Interest is held longer when children actively participate with words or motions.

4. Is the *author's style* enjoyable?

   a. Is the book written clearly with a vocabulary and sequence the child can understand?

   b. Are repetitions of words, actions, rhymes, or story parts used? Anticipated repetition is part of the young child's enjoyment of stories.

   c. Does the story develop and end with a satisfying climax of events?

Fig. 6-3 Many early childhood books have large colorful pictures.

   d. Are there humorous parts or silly names? The young child's humor is often slapstick in nature. (Pie-in-the-face, all fall down type rather than play on words)

5. Does it have *educational value?*

   a. Could you use it to expand knowledge in any way?

   b. Does it offer new vocabulary? Does it increase or broaden understanding?

Some books meet all criteria of the established standards, others only a few. The age of the children make some criteria more important than others. Schools often select books to buy with sturdiness and price in mind.

READING BOOKS

Teachers read books in both indoor and outdoor settings, to one child or many. If a child asks for a story and a teacher is available, the book is shared. Planned reading called storytimes are also part of a quality early childhood program.

Building positive attitudes takes skill. A step-by-step outline is helpful.

Step 1. Read the book to yourself enough times to develop a feeling for characters and the story line.

Step 2. Arrange a setting with the children's and teacher's comfort in mind. The illustrations should be at children's eye level. Seating arrangements are chosen for 5-15 minute seating. Some teachers prefer small chairs for both children and teachers, others prefer rug areas. Avoid traffic paths and noise interruptions.

Step 3. Make a *motivational* introductory statement. A motivational statement should create a desire to listen or encourage listening.

"There's a boy in this book who wanted to give his mother a birthday present."

"Monkeys can be funny, and they are funny in this book."

"Have you ever wondered where animals go at night to sleep?"

"On the last page of this book is a picture of a happy monster. Are monsters real or make-believe?"

Step 4. Hold the book to either your left or right side. With your hand in place, make both sides of the page visible. Keep the book at children's eye level, figure 6-4.

Step 5. Begin reading; try to glance at the sentences and turn to meet the children's eyes as often as possible so your voice goes to the children. Also watch for body reactions. Speak clearly, using a rate of speed which enables the children to both look at illustrations and hear what you are reading. Enjoy the story with the children by being enthusiastic. Dramatize and emphasize key parts of the story but not to the degree the children are watching you and not the book. Change your voice to suit the characters if you feel comfortable doing so. A good story will hold attention, and often stimulates comments or questions. Answer and discuss them, approvingly. If you feel that interruptions are decreasing the enjoyment for other children, ask a child to wait until the end when you will be glad to discuss it. Then do it. If on the other hand, most of the group is interested, take the time to discuss an idea. Sometimes children suck their thumbs or act sleepy during reading times. They seem to connect

Fig. 6-4 Both sides of the page are visible and at the children's eye level.

books with bedtime; many parents read to their children at this time. By watching closely while reading you will be able to tell if you still have the attention of the children. You can sometimes draw a child back to the book with a direct question like, "Debbie, can you see the cat's tail?"

Step 6. You may want to ask a few discussion questions at the end of the book. Questions can clear up ideas, encourage use of vocabulary words, pinpoint parts that were especially enjoyed. You will have to decide whether to read more than one book at one time. It helps to remember how long your group of children can sit before getting restless. Storytimes should end on an enthusiastic note, with the child looking forward to another story.

CARE AND STORAGE

By setting an example and making clear statements about handling books, the teacher can help children form good book-care habits. However, with time and use, even the sturdiest books will need repairs.

Books that are part of a school's collection should be stored at eye level in an upright position where they are easily attainable.

Fig. 6-5 A soft rug, pillows or chairs for sitting make this an inviting book corner.

Table and chairs close by the bookshelf invite looking at books, figure 6-5. Reading centers provide a degree of quiet and comfort where a child can enjoy a book alone or with other children.

SUMMARY

Three goals of reading books to the young child are:

- For enjoyment and attitude development.

- For knowledge.

- For development of listening and other skills.

A careful selection of books makes it easier to reach these goals, and gives reading activities a greater chance for success.

A teacher who is prepared can interact with enthusiasm by showing her own enjoyment; this promotes language growth.

SUGGESTED ACTIVITIES

- Select, prepare and present three books to children. Record what you believe are your strong and weak points.

- Read a children's book to two classmates and have each one evaluate the presentation.

- Visit the local library. Select five books you feel are suitable for use. Tell how they match the selection criteria.

- A suggested list of children's books is included in the appendix. Develop your own book list using short descriptions, as follows.

    Zion, Gene, <u>Harry the Dirty Dog</u>, Harper and Row, Pub. About a family dog who gets so dirty his family doesn't recognize him.

- Make a list of 5 nonfiction books that could be used with preschoolers.

REVIEW

1. Read the following descriptions of comments by a teacher who is reading to children. Select those comments which you feel would help the child accomplish a goal mentioned in this unit.

    a. "Sit down now and stop talking, it's storytime."

    b. "Kathy, can you remember how the mouse got out of the trap?"

    c. "What part of this story made you laugh?"

    d. "John, I can't read any more because you've made Lonnie cry by stepping on her hand. Children, storytime is over."

    e. "Children don't look out the window, look at the book. Children, the book is more interesting than that storm."

    f. "Donald, big boys don't tear book pages."

    g. "Was the dog striped or spotted? If you can't answer then you weren't listening."

    h. "Mary, of course you liked the story, everyone did."

    i. "Tell me Mario, what was the boy's name in our story? I'm going to sit here until you tell me."

    j. "No, the truck wasn't green, Luci. Children tell Luci what color the truck was."

    k. "Take your thumb out of your mouth, Debbie; it's storytime."

    l. "I like the way you all watched the book and told me what was in each picture."

    m. "One book's enough, we can't sit here all day you know."

    n. "Children we have to finish this book before we can go outside, sit back down."

    o. "That book had lots of colorful pictures to look at."

    p. "Well, now we found out who can help us if we ever lose mama in a store."

2. Answer the following questions:

    a. Why is it important to read a child's book before it is read to the children?

    b. How can a child care assistant help children learn how books are used to find answers?

    c. Why should teachers watch for the young child's reactions to the story while she is reading?

3. Select the phrase in Column II which applies to the item in Column I.

1. Fairy tales.

2. First step in planned reading.

3. Arrange setting with comfort in mind.

4. Stop storytelling to discuss it.

5. Not appropriate for early childhood level.

6. Children become restless after twenty-five minutes.

7. Directly quoted conversation.

8. "And I'll huff and I'll puff and I'll blow your house down."

9. "So they all had a party with the cookies and milk." The End.

10. "The rabbit's just like me, I can run real fast."

11. A book should be read and held.

12. Books are more inviting when stored this way.

a. Before teacher starts reading to the group.

b. When children show interest in a subject.

c. A book about war and killing.

d. Book may not be appropriate for this age level.

e. May be too frightening.

f. "Tick-tock," said the clock.

g. Teacher reads the book beforehand.

h. Repetition in the Three Little Pigs.

i. Identification.

j. A satisfying climax to a story.

k. In an upright position with the front cover showing.

l. At children's eye level.

unit 7 storytelling

OBJECTIVES

After studying this unit, the student should be able to

- Describe how storytelling can help language growth.
- List teacher techniques in storytelling.
- Demonstrate the ability to create a story which meets suggested criteria.

Storytelling is an art which child care staff members can develop and use to increase a child's enjoyment of language. When good stories are told, the child listens intently; words and ideas are conceived when there is a close contact with an enthusiastic adult, figure 7-1. Storytelling enables the teacher to share herself and her life experiences in an individual way.

The teacher's face, gestures, words and voice tone tell the story when books or pictures are not used. Eye contact is held throughout storytelling period. The child makes his own mental pictures as the plot unfolds.

SOURCES

A story idea can be found in books, children's magazines, films, story records, or from another storyteller. A story idea can be self-created.

Storytelling may occur at almost any time during the course of the day, inside or outside. No books or props are necessary. The child care assistant is free to relate the story in her own words and manner. Children will show by their actions what parts of the story are of high interest. The storyteller can increase their enjoyment by emphasizing these features.

A teacher-created story can fill a void. In any group of young children there are special interests and problems. Stories can expand interests and give the child more information on a subject. Some problems can be solved by the stories and conversations which take place.

Although a new teacher may have little confidence in her storytelling abilities, the application of some techniques for selecting, creating and telling stories will almost insure success. This, together with the experience of presenting stories to children, should convince the child care assistant student that storytelling is enjoyable to preschoolers, and is rewarding to the teacher.

SELECTION

The selection of a story is as important as the selection of a book. The following criteria is commonly used:

Fig. 7-1 An enthusiastic storyteller gets interest and delighted responses.

- Age level appropriateness.

    Is the story told in simple, easily understood words? Is it familiar in light of the child's life experiences?

    Is it frightening? Can the child profit from the values of the characters?

- Real characters.

    Is there good development of characters in the story? Are the personalities clearly presented? Are they believable and consistent?

- Plot.

    Does the setting create a stage for what is to come?

    Is there action?

    Something of interest to resolve?

    A start where something happens?

    A building to a climax? Maybe some suspense?

    A timely, satisfying conclusion?

    Are characters introduced as they appear?

- Style.

    Is there repetition or rhyme?

    Silly words or a surprise ending?

    Directly quoted conversations?

    Child involvement with speaking or movements?

    A mood which helps the plot develop?

- Storyteller enthusiasm.

    Can the story be well liked by the teller?

    Does the teller feel "at home" with it?

STORY IDEAS

Teachers sometimes begin by telling stories from printed sources. Many classic stories have delighted children in every generation. The following are some examples.

Classic Tales

Goldilocks and the Three Bears
Little Red Riding Hood
The Three Little Pigs
Billy Goats Gruff
The Little Red Hen
The Gingerbread Boy
Jack and the Beanstalk

From Aesop's Fables:

The Lion and the Mouse
The Shepherd Boy and Wolf
The Hare and the Tortoise
The Ant and the Grasshopper
The Wind and the Sun

Traditional stories:

Hans Christian Andersen, *Ugly Duckling*
      The Emperor's New Clothes
Wanda Gag, *Millions of Cats*
Beatrix Potter, *The Tale of Peter Rabbit*
Marjorie Flack, *Angus and the Ducks*
Rudyard Kipling, *Just So Stories*

TECHNIQUES

Before presenting a story, the child care assistant should be familiar with the techniques of good storytelling:

- Know the story well, but not word for word. Become familiar with the key ideas. Know the key happenings and their order of appearance in the story.

- Practice before a mirror or with another staff member.

- Enjoy and live the story as you tell it in your own words. Use gestures.

- Maintain eye contact; watch for children's interest or restlessness.

- Pace the storytelling by going faster during exciting or fast action parts and slower in serious parts.

- Use a clear, firm voice; try altering your voice volume to fit the story. Your voice can get down to almost a whisper if the story calls for it. Change your voice to fit characters when they speak.

- Involve the children periodically, especially with repetitions, rhymes or actions, silly words, or appropriate questions.

- Sit close to the group; make sure all are comfortable before you begin.

Even the best of storytellers has an occasional flop. If the storyteller senses the children are restless, the story may be concluded very quickly. Storytelling may be tried at a later time using a revised version or a new story.

CREATING STORIES

When creating a new story, practice it so that it can be retold in a similar fashion the next time. File cards can be used to jot down the title, beginning, middle, and ending key ideas for future reference. Bad guys in stories are enjoyed as well as good guys. Some teachers find that a popular character in one story can have further adventures in the next. Having a problem to be resolved serves as the basis for many well-known classics. As teachers use their own stories they tend to cut and add to them based on the reaction of the children.

STORIES FOR STORYTELLING

The following stories can be used by the beginning student.

The Little House with No Doors and No Windows and a Star Inside

Author Unknown

Plan to have an apple and a knife ready for the ending. A plate full of apple slices is sometimes enjoyed after the story.

Once there was a little boy who had played almost all day. He had played with all his toys and all the games he knew, and he could not think of anything else to do. So he went to his mother who always knew the nicest things for a child to do. He said, "Mother what shall I do now?"

His mother said, "I know about a little red house with no doors and no windows and a star inside. You can find it, if you go look for it."

So the little boy went outside and there he met a little girl. He said, "Do you know where there is a little red house with no doors and no windows and a star inside?"

The little girl said, "No, I don't know where there is a little red house with no doors and no windows and a star inside, but you ask my daddy. He is a farmer and he knows lots of things. He's down by the barn and maybe he can help you."

So the little boy went to the farmer down by the barn and said, "Do you know where there is a little red house with no doors and no windows, and a star inside?"

"No," said the farmer, "I don't know, but why don't you ask grandmother. She is in her house up on the hill. She is very wise and knows many things. Maybe she can help you."

So the little boy went up the hill to grandmother's and asked, "Do you know where there is a little red house with no doors and no windows and a star inside?" "No," said Grandmother, "I don't know, but you ask the wind, for the wind goes everywhere, and I am sure he can help you."

So the little boy went outside and asked the wind, "Do you know where I can find a little red house with no doors and no windows and a star inside?" And the wind said, "OHHH! OOOOOO OOOOOO!" And it sounded to the little boy as if the wind said, "Come with me." So the little boy ran after the wind. He ran through the grass and into the orchard and there on the ground he found the little house . . the little red house with no doors and no windows and a star inside! He picked it up and it filled both his hands. He ran home to his mother and said, "Look, Mother! I found the little red house with no doors and no windows, but I cannot see the star!"

So this is what his mother did. (cuts apple) "Now I see the star!" said the little boy. (to children) DO YOU?, figure 7-2.

Laughing Stock & Gastly

by Sister Carol Bettencourt

There was a family of elephants that lived in the jungle – there were very large mama and papa elephants – and smaller baby elephants; and they were all the color grey – all except one – his name was Laughing Stock, he got his name because all the other elephants had never seen an elephant the color of Laughing Stock. He was the color orange! Have you ever seen an orange elephant? Poor Laughing Stock, everyone made fun of him because he was so different.

In the same jungle, also, lived a family of giraffes – oh, they were so tall and so nice-looking with their yellow and brown bodies. One day, Laughing Stock was going for a walk when he saw the giraffes eating the leaves

right from the top of the trees – those giraffes certainly were tall.

"Hi giraffes," said Laughing Stock! "Hi elephant," said the giraffes! "Say elephant," shouted one of the giraffes, "you don't look like an elephant – your body is the color orange." Then all the giraffes started to laugh. Poor Laughing Stock. One of the giraffes, still laughing loudly, said, "you and Gastly would make a fine pair!" "Who's Gastly," asked the elephant? "I am," said a quiet little voice. Laughing Stock looked around but didn't see anyone except for the giraffes – then, he saw something move and Laughing Stock looked closely into the green bushes. Wha wha wha wha you you (poor Laughing Stock was having a hard time making the words come out). You're green! I've I've I've never seen a green giraffe before! "Neither have we," laughed the other giraffes. "Oh, but I think you're pretty," said Laughing Stock. "You do?" said Gastly. "Thank you, no one ever said that to me before." "You're welcome," smiled Laughing Stock, and right away they became

Fig. 7-2 "The little red house with the star inside. Do you see the star?"

Fig. 7-3 If children's attention is focused elsewhere, it may not be a good time for storytelling.

good friends and each one helped the other. And because they were friends, it didn't hurt so much when others laughed at them, because they had someone who liked them just the way they were.

This story leads well into discussions about color. Can you find something in the room the same color as Laughing Stock? As Gastly? Also about likeness and differences:

Is your hair the same color as one of your friends?
Can you think of something that makes you different?
Do your friends look just like you?

Other suggested stories for storytelling can be found in the appendix.

The student child care assistant develops an individual style through telling stories and watching children's reactions. Although props need not be used, there are times when a toy boat, cowboy hat, or other object may help focus children's attention and add to the storytelling experience. Since younger preschoolers concentrate on concrete "real" objects and happenings, storytelling may not be able to hold their attention as well as the older preschool child, figure 7-3.

SUMMARY

The prime goals of storytelling are a feeling of togetherness and enjoyment through the words of a story. Building listening skills, vocabulary development and expanded interest are others.

Child care assistants can find stories from printed sources and from other teachers. They are urged to create their own. By following suggested techniques and criteria, a successful activity for both children and teachers is possible.

Stories are told in the teacher's own words with key happenings well in mind. Watching the children's interest and reactions keeps the teacher aware of how well the experience is accepted. Any skill takes practice. Storytelling skills become better with use.

SUGGESTED ACTIVITIES

- Create a story. In outline form write the beginning, middle, and ending. Practice it on a fellow student. Use your own title or select one of the following.

> The Giant Ice Cream Cone
> Magic Shoes
> The Dog Who Wouldn't Bark
> Billy Found a Dollar
> The Big Birthday Present
> The Mouse Who Chased Cats
> The Policeman and Mike
> The Fastest Bike
> I've Got a Bug in My Pocket

- Tell a story to a group of children.

> What parts interested the children the most?
> What would you change if you told it again?
> What techniques were used to hold interest?

- Invite a librarian or experienced teacher who tells stories during story hours to share her favorite stories with the class.

- Tell a story and have it recorded on video tape. Play it back. Look for strong points and weaknesses.

- Listen to a commercial storytelling record. List the techniques used to hold the child's interest.

REVIEW

A. The first column lists common preschool characteristics. Select the appropriate storytelling techniques and criteria from the second column.

I	II
1. Likes to move frequently.	a. Selects stories without cruel monsters or vivid descriptions of accidents.
2. Has had experiences at home, school and in the community.	
3. Has fear of large animals and bodily hurt.	b. "Ducky-Ducky and Be-Bop-Boo went to the park to meet Moo-Moo the Cow."
4. Likes play with words.	c. Stories contain familiar objects and animals.
5. Likes to be part of the group.	d. "What did the big bird say to the baby bird?"
6. Likes to talk.	e. "Help Tipper blow out the candle. Pretend my finger is a candle and try to blow it out!"
	f. "Stand up and reach for the moon like Johnny did. Good. Now close your eyes, is it dark like night? You couldn't reach the moon, but can you find your nose with your eyes closed?"

B. Briefly answer the following questions.

1. Why should storytelling take place often in early childhood centers?

2. What are some possible problems of a young child that a story might help solve?

3. How can the teacher bring about the learning of words and facts through storytelling?

4. Name three resources for stories.

C.   Select the correct answers. Each item has more than one correct answer.

1. In storytelling, the storyteller not only uses words but also the
    a. hands.
    b. face.
    c. eyes.
    d. gestures.

2. Recommended techniques used by storytellers of young children are:
    a. changing the voice to fit the character.
    b. changing the personality of a character during the story.
    c. stopping without ending a story so that children will listen quietly the next time.
    d. watching children closely and emphasizing the parts they enjoy.

3. Criteria for story selection include
    a. real, believable characters.
    b. a plot with lots of action.
    c. a possible problem to be resolved.
    d. one that can be memorized.

4. Teacher should not
    a. let children be inattentive during their story.
    b. feel defeated if a story occasionally flops.
    c. put bad guys in stories.
    d. tell the story word for word

5. During storytelling time,
    a. the child can form his own mental pictures.
    b. the child care assistant can share interesting personal life experiences.
    c. the child care assistant models being creative with words.
    d. the child care assistant models correct speech.

unit 8 poetry

OBJECTIVES

After studying this unit, the student should be able to

- Explain the value of poetry.
- Demonstrate the ability to present a poem.
- Create a poem with features which appeal to young children.

Poetry is an enjoyable method of developing listening skills.

GOALS

Activities which involve poetry hold many opportunities to promote language development, and associate pleasure with words. By identifying with poetry, children can quickly feel at home with their imaginary pictures.

In addition to fast action and mood building, there is the joy of the rhythm and beat of the words. Some rhythms in classic rhymes are so strong that they can produce body movements or clapping. The nursery rhyme "Jack and Jill" or "Twinkle, Twinkle, Little Star," are good examples. Not only are poems of this type appealing, they also paint vivid mental images. Other poems appeal to the emotions, figure 8-1.

Fig. 8-1 Some poetry brings laughter.

LEARNINGS

Poetry provides an opportunity for a child to learn new words, ideas and attitudes, and experience life through the eyes of the author. Many of us still know how many days there are in a month by remembering a simple poem we learned as a child. If you are asked to say the alphabet, the classic ABC song of childhood may come to mind.

Poetry has form and order. It is dependable. It is also easy to learn. Simple rhymes are picked up quickly, as most mothers have learned from their child's ability to pick up television commercials. Children in early childhood centers enjoy the accomplishment of memorizing a short verse. They may ask to share these poems they have learned with the teacher, just as they ask to sing songs they know. A song may be a poem put to music.

The teacher should provide the child who responds to poetry with encouragement, attention, and a positive comment. As with reading, storytelling and other language activities, the goal of the child care assistant is to offer children pleasure and enjoyment of the language arts while expanding the child's knowledge and interest.

Poetry, then, is used for a variety of reasons.

- To train the ear and experience the pleasure of hearing sounds.
- To provide enjoyment by silly words, fun, and humor.

- To stimulate the imagination.
- To increase vocabulary and knowledge.
- To build self-worth and give a feeling of self-confidence.

TEACHER TECHNIQUES

The teacher selects poems which she can enjoy and present with enthusiasm. Pictures or illustrations can be used in poetry presentation to add eye interest and help children focus on words, figure 8-2. Other props which relate to the poem (such as a teddy bear or policeman's hat) will gain attention. Some of the best collections of poems have no pictures; others have a large illustration with one poem per page.

A poem can be enjoyed indoors or outdoors, in a train, car or bus, or between activities as a fill-in when teacher or children are waiting.

The teacher should have read, practiced and possibly memorized the poem beforehand, so it may be offered easily — without stops and hesitation. Most teachers have a few favorite poems memorized.

Posting poems on bulletin boards creates interest. A poetry tree can be made by placing a tree limb in plaster of paris. Poems written on the back of paper leaves can be hung on the tree. Every day a child can be chosen to pick the poem of the day.

Young children sometimes create their own rhymes. A child care assistant can jot them down for display or to be taken home as a "poem authored by Robby."

Poetry activities need sensitive handling. Children may recite a favorite poem together. A teacher can suggest "Let's say it together," but a child should not be singled out or forced to recite.

SOURCES

Collections of children's poetry are available at the public library. Children's magazines and teachers' magazines are another source. The child care assistant can create poetry from her own experience. The following suggestions for creating poems for young children can help the teacher by pointing out the especially enjoyable features found in popular classics.

- Mental images are found in every line.

- Strong rhythms bring out an urge to chant, move or sing.

- Frequent rhyming occurs.

- Action verbs are used often.

- Each line has an independent thought.

- A move and change in rhythm are present.

- Words are within their understanding level.

- Themes and subjects are familiar to the young child.

SUGGESTED POEMS

The poems which follow are examples of poems which appeal to the young child.

Fig. 8-2 Poetry can be presented with flannelboard cutouts.

IF I WERE AN APPLE

If I were an apple
And grew on a tree,
I think I'd drop down
On a nice boy like me.

I wouldn't stay there
Giving nobody joy;
I'd fall down at once
And say, "Eat me, my boy!"

— Old Rhyme

RAIN

Rain, Rain, hurry. Scurry.
Make a puddle. Patter. Spatter.
Get me wet. It doesn't matter.
I've pulled rain boots on my feet
So I can splish-splash in the street.
My yellow slicker's slippery-new.
I'm all dressed up, Rain, just for you.

Anne Alexander

(Reprinted by permission from The Christian Science Monitor
©The Christian Science Publishing Society, All rights reserved)

This poem is usually presented with pictures cut from magazines.

Alphabet Rhyme

Aa is for apple	*Nn is for nickel*
Bb is for ball	*Oo is for olive*
Cc is for cat	*Pp is for pickle*
Dd is for doll	*Qq is for quilt*
Ee is for egg	*Rr is for rose*
Ff is for frog	*Ss is for snail*
Gg is for gum	*Tt is for toes*
Hh is for hog	*Uu is for umbrella*
Ii is for ice	*Vv is for vine*
Jj is for jam	*Ww is for window*
Kk is for kite and	*Xx just won't rhyme*
Ll is for lamb	*Yy is for yellow*
Mm is for mouse	*Zz is for zipper*

Buttons are fine
But a zipper is quicker.

Jeanne M. Machado

Examples of concept-building questions are:

Which ones can you eat?

Could you play with any?

How many have tails? Let's count.

Which are smaller than you?

Do any have eyes?

Can some make a noise?

POEMS BY CHILD CARE ASSISTANT STUDENTS

Most of the following are poems written by students who created them to use with young children. These beginning attempts show that most teachers are capable of writing enjoyable and interesting poetry to use for language development.

A SLEEPY PLACE TO BE

Oh, it was a yawning day
That nobody wanted to work or play
And everybody felt the very same way.

There was a duckling who quacked and quacked
He had soft down upon his back.
He was tired of swimming and everything,
So he put his head down under his wing.
And there under the shadowy shade tree
He slept until it was half-past three.

A little old pig gave a big loud squeal
As he ate every scrap of his noonday meal.
And under the shadowy shade tree
He slept as quietly as could be.

A butterfly blue, green and red
Sat with her wings above her head
Up on a branch of the shadowy tree.
Oh, what a sleepy place to be.

Debbie Lauer

A POEM FOR THE SENSES

My nose can be my friend sometimes
But other times it's not.
Because some things are good to smell
And some things are not!

My ears can hear all kinds of sounds
And some are very nice.
But to the things I like to hear
I want to listen twice.

I like to feel things with my hands
And with my fingers too.
By touching things I learn a lot
There is so much to do.

I like to eat all kinds of fruit,
It's good to taste and chew
Vegetables, meat, and dairy foods too
Are also very good for you.

My eyes can see all kinds of things
And all I do is look,
But I have to focus with my eyes
To see printing in a book.

Liz Adrian

LITTLE KITTY

Pretty little Kitty
With fur so soft and sweet,
You tiptoe oh so softly
On your tiny little feet.

Fluffy little Kitty
With eyes so big and round,
I never hear you coming,
You hardly make a sound.

Silly little Kitty
Playing with a ball.
Listen! Someone's coming!
You scamper down the hall.

Lazy little Kitty,
Tiny sleepy head,
Curled up, sleeping soundly
In your cozy little bed.

Bari Morgan

DOG TALK

Oh what fun it would be
To see that cat run up the tree.
Woof, woof, woof.

See them scamper, see them scurry
To run and hide in a hurry.
Woof!, Woof!, Woof!

Is that another dog I see
By gosh, he's a lot bigger than me.
Yike!, Yike!, Yike!

Jeanne M. Machado

SUMMARY

Poetry can be a source of enjoyment and learning for young children. The rhythm, word images, fast action and rhyme are used to promote listening skill.

Short verses, easily remembered, give self-confidence with words. Encouragement and attention is offered by the child care assistant when the child's interest is present.

Poems are selected and practiced for enthusiastic, smooth presentations. They can be selected from various sources or created by the teacher. Props help children focus on words. Poems are created or selected, keeping in mind the features which attract and interest young children.

SUGGESTED ACTIVITIES

• Select five poems from any source. Be ready to state the reasons you selected them when you bring them to the next class meeting.

• Make a list of ten books that include children's poetry. Cite author, title, publisher and copyright date.

• Create a poem for young children. Go back and review the features most often found in classic rhymes.

• Present a poem to a group of preschoolers. Evaluate its success in a few sentences.

REVIEW

A.   Name a few reasons why poetry is used with young children.

B.   From Column II select the terms which go with the items in Column I.

I	II
1. Poetry	a. An action verb
2. Rhyme	b. Self-confidence
3. Beat	c. A rhythmic measure
4. Order and form	d. Mental pictures
5. Images	e. Words ending in alike sounds
6. Remembered	f. Consistent and dependable
7. Interest	g. Teacher attention
8. Goal	h. After practice
9. Presentation	i. Enjoyment
10. Reciting	j. Promotes listening skill
11. Classics	k. Never forced
12. Song	l. Library
13. Props	m. Mother Goose rhymes
14. Run	n. Musical poem
15. Source	o. Focus attention

unit 9 visual activities

OBJECTIVES

After studying this unit the student should be able to

- Describe flannelboards and types of flannelboard activities.
- Make and present three flannelboard activities.
- List visual aids that can be used to develop listening ability.

For the child care assistant teacher, flannelboard activities are a rewarding experience. The attention of young children is easily captured. The assistant teacher finds the use of flannelboard activities highly popular and effective. The children literally sit on the edge of their chairs during storytelling, straining to see and hear, looking forward to the next piece to be put on the flannelboard, figure 9-1.

Stories to be used with flannelboard activities, are selected by the same criteria as for storytelling, see page 49 (Unit 7). In addition to stories, poetry and songs, other listening and learning activities can be presented with flannelboards.

FLANNELBOARD CONSTRUCTION

Boards of different sizes, shapes and designs are used, depending on the needs of the center. They may be propped up in the chalkboard tray, on a chair, or on an easel. Boards can be covered on both sides using a different color for each side. Many are made by covering a sheet of heavy cardboard, display board, styrofoam, or wood with a piece of solid-colored flannel yardage, figure 9-2. Stores which sell school supplies have premade boards which vary in price.

Flannel and felt are popular, but some other materials also work well. Almost all fuzzy-textured material is usable. It is a good idea to press a small piece of felt or pellon to a fabric to see how well it sticks before buying the fabric.

Some boards have pocket charts in the back so flannel pieces to be used can be lined up and ready beforehand. There are also childhood centers which have part of the walls or dividers covered with flannel or felt.

Fig. 9-1 Young children's attention is easily captured by flannelboard stories.

Fig. 9-2 The children are placing pellon story pieces on a board covered with flannel.

Wire mesh inserted beneath the fabric makes it possible to use magnetic pieces on the board. Display fabrics to which three-dimensional objects will adhere are available at commercial audiovisual companies. Special adhesives and tape are needed for this type of flannelboard.

ACTIVITY SETS

Pieces for flannel activity sets can be made in a number of ways and from a number of fabrics and materials. Pellon and felt, because of their low cost and durability, are the most popular. Paper figures with flannel backing also stick well. Commercial tapes, sandpaper and fuzzy velour paper are other possibilities. Premade flannelboard sets are available at school supply stores, figure 9-3.

Shapes and figures can be traced from books, magazines, coloring books or other sources. Tracing paper is helpful for this purpose. Color can be added with felt pen markers, oil pastels, embroidery pens, crayons, and colored pencils. Sets take time to make but are well worth the trouble. Favorites may be presented over and over again.

Proper storage and care will preserve the pieces thus prolonging their usefulness. A flat box, or large mailing envelope or manila folder is practical for storage. If pieces become bent, a warm iron makes them flat again.

Fig. 9-3 A commercial flannelboard is in use here.

Like most listening activities, a semi-secluded comfortable area is chosen for presentation as it requires that the teacher speaks, places pieces on the board in proper sequence, and focuses on the children's reactions. This is hard to do if the story or activity is not well in mind. Since pieces are usually added one at a time, the child care assistant should keep them in an open flat box or manila folder in her lap, or behind the board stacked in order of their appearance. A child care assistant periodically checks to see if the set has all its pieces, particularly in large centers where many staff members use the same sets. She makes new pieces whenever necessary. New sets are appreciated by the entire staff, and can be developed with the needs and interests of a particular group of children in mind.

In addition to storytelling activities, sets may be used for songs, poetry, numbers, language development, and thinking activities.

PRESENTATION

In order to present activities with ease, the following steps should be noted for the beginner:

- Read story and check pieces to be used.
- Practice until a smooth coordination of words and placing pieces on the board is possible.
- Set up the flannelboard.
- Check and prepare pieces in order of their appearance.
- Place pieces out of view.
- Gather children.
- Introduce with a motivation statement, if desired.
- Tell the story, watching for reactions from the children.
- Discuss for language development.
- Keep pieces flat. Store.

SUGGESTED STORIES AND ACTIVITIES

Resources for story ideas are plentiful. Stories created by child care assistants may be enjoyed as much as commercial sets and classic stories. Sets can promote listening, vocabulary development, concept development, often within one activity. The visual shapes or pieces are linked to words and ideas.

The following activities and stories are suggested as a start for the beginning teacher. They may also be used to add variety and ideas for new sets. Patterns for the pieces can be found in the Appendix, page 137. Additional flannelboard stories and patterns may be found in the Appendix also.

THE LION AND THE MOUSE

— Unknown. A classic story.

Pieces:

Lion sleeping	Rope
Lion awake	Mouse
Tree	2 Hunters

On the board, place the sleeping lion next to tree. Place mouse on lion's back, moving him slowly while speaking in a soft voice.

There once was a little mouse who saw a big lion sleeping by a tree. "Oh, it would be fun to climb on top of the lion, and slide down his tail," thought the mouse. So — quietly he tiptoed close to the lion. When he climbed on the lion's back, the fur felt so soft and warm between his toes that he began running up and down the lion's back.

The lion awoke. He felt a tickle up on his back. He opened one eye, and saw the little mouse, which he then caught in his paw.

Move mouse under lion's paw.

"Let me go — please!" said the mouse. "I'm sorry I woke you from your nap. Let me go, and I'll never bother you again. Maybe you and I could be friends — friends help each other you know."

This made the lion laugh, "A little mouse like you, help me! I'm big, I'm strong, and I'm brave!" Then the lion laughed again, and he let the mouse go.

Take mouse off.

The mouse ran away, and he didn't see the lion for a long time. But one day when the mouse was out looking for seeds for dinner he saw the lion tied to a tree with a rope, and two hunters near him.

Remove sleeping lion. Add awake lion, placing next to tree with rope on top.

One hunter said, "Well, this rope will hold the lion until we can go get our truck, and take him to the zoo." So the hunters walked away.

The mouse ran up to the lion as soon as the hunters were out of sight. He said, "Hello lion."

Add mouse.

The lion answered, "Well, I guess it's your turn to laugh at me tied to this tree."

"I'm not going to laugh" said the mouse, as he quickly started to chew on the rope.

Move mouse close to rope. Remove rope.

The mouse chewed, and chewed, and chewed. The rope fell apart, and the lion was free.

"You are a good friend," said the lion.

"Hop on my back, hold on, let's get away from here before those two hunters come back."

Place lion in running position with mouse on lion's back.

"OK," said the mouse. "I'd like that."

So you see sometimes little friends can help big friends. The size of a friend isn't really too important.

THE SEED — by Margie Cowsert

(Written while a student. An example of a teacher-created story)

Pieces:	Seed	Bird	
Small roots	**Small trunk**	**Large trunk**
Green shoot	**Leaves**	**Large leaves**
Deer	**Beaver**	**Large roots**
Mr. Man	**Apples (5 or 6 or more)**	

Once upon a time there was a seed named Abraham. He didn't know what kind of plant he would be so he asked Mr. Bird. Mr. Bird didn't know, but wanted to eat Abraham. Abraham asked him to wait until after he found out what he would be and the bird agreed to wait.

Abraham grew small roots and green shoots. He asked Mr. Deer if he knew what he would grow up to be. "Do you know what I'll be when I grow up?" Mr. Deer said "No" but wanted to eat the tender green shoot. Abraham said "Please wait," so Mr. Deer decided to wait.

Abraham grew a small trunk and leaves. He was glad he was a tree but still didn't know what kind. He asked Mr. Beaver, "Do you know what I'll be when I grow up?" Mr. Beaver didn't know but wanted to eat Abraham's tender bark. He decided to wait also.

Abraham grew big roots, a big trunk and more leaves, but still didn't know what kind of tree he was. He asked Mr. Man, "Do you know what I'll be when I grow up?" Mr. Man didn't know but he wanted to chop down Abraham to make a house. He decided to wait.

Abraham grew apples. Hurray! He knew now that he was an apple tree. He told Mr. Bird he could eat him now. Mr. Bird said Abraham was too big but that he would like one of the apples. Mr. Deer thought the tree was too big too, but he did want an apple. Mr. Beaver wanted an apple. Mr. Man wanted an apple too.

Abraham Apple Tree was so happy to know what he was and that no one was going to eat him or chop him down, that he grew lots of apples.

OTHER VISUAL AIDS

Children's magazines contain many ideas and stories which a child care assistant can share with young children. Magazine activities can be adapted for the young child; in many cases they are written for elementary school pupils.

Hand and finger puppets are used to focus the children's attention to listening activities. The puppets can be used to introduce an activity, or they may be kept in the teacher's pocket to be used throughout the day.

Other visual aids are films, filmstrips, slides, photographs, and transparencies for use with overhead projectors. Some programs have these aids available, while others do not. If they are available, a child care assistant should be able to operate the equipment, use and care for it properly. Planning activities using audiovisual machines can bring both variety and an opportunity for further listening experiences. Most schools have a staff member available to train the beginning assistant in both care and use.

Pictures and photographs are valuable teaching aids for listening and vocabulary development. Hearing a word for the first time and having a visual model makes learning easier and faster. Being able to experience the real thing is best of all, but pictures and photographs are many times more practical and possible than firsthand experiences with the young child. Therefore, they are used often when the actual subject is not available to widen a child's view of the world.

SUMMARY

Flannelboard presentations are one of the most popular and successful listening activities for the young child. Stories are told while figures and shapes are put in view. The children can learn new ideas and words by seeing the visual model, while listening to the story.

Child care assistants practice presentations until the activity flows smoothly with words and pieces while the children's behaviors are being noted. Flannelboard activities in many other learning areas besides language development take place in early childhood centers.

A wide variety of fabrics are available for both boards and pieces; felt and flannel are the most commonly used for boards.

Other visual aids found in early childhood centers and used to develop listening skills are:

- Pictures and photographs

- Films and filmstrips

- Slides

- Overhead and opaque projectors

- Tape recorders

- Listening center headsets

- Language master

SUGGESTED ACTIVITIES

- Visit a center to watch a flannelboard presentation or invite a practicing teacher to present an activity to the class.

- Give a presentation to a small group of classmates. The classmates should make helpful suggestions in written form while watching the presentation, trying to look at the presentations through the eyes of a child.

- Write an original story for the flannelboard on a ditto master. These ditto masters can be purchased from a stationery or office supply store. Include patterns for your pieces, also put these on a ditto master.

- If videotape equipment is available in your classroom, give a flannelboard presentation and evaluate yourself.

- Bring in a children's magazine which either suggests a listening activity or contains a section or page you feel could be used as a listening activity. Discuss the activity with the class.

- Plan an activity involving audiovisual equipment you have never used before.

- Make three flannelboard sets using any materials you wish.

- Invite an audiovisual technician from a local school district, college or university to speak on the operation and care of audiovisual equipment, or visit an audiovisual department.

REVIEW

1. Name the types of materials usable in board construction.

2. Name the kinds of fabrics from which flannelboard pieces can be made.

3. In your opinion, what is the best way to color pieces for flannelboards?

4. Why is the use of visual aids valuable?

5. Place in correct order. (You may want to use one number more than once)

    a. Give a flannelboard presentation.

    b. Set up area with board.

    c. Check pieces.

    d. Practice.

    e. Place pieces in order of appearance.

    f. Gather children.

    g. Place pieces out of sight.

    h. Discuss what happened during the activity with children.

    i. Store set by keeping pieces flat.

    j. Introduce the set with a motivational statement if you wish.

Section 3 Speaking — A Language Art

unit 10 realizing goals

OBJECTIVES

After studying this unit, the student should be able to

- State five goals of planned speech activities.
- Describe appropriate teacher behavior in daily conversation with children.
- Give three examples of questioning techniques.

A child has many opportunities to learn to speak. While some activities are planned, others just happen. The action happens along with words, figure 10-1.

To help develop each child's speaking ability, schools base their plans upon goals. All staff members should use these goals as a guide for planning a variety of daily learning experiences.

Activities can be classed into two groups — structured and unstructured. Structured activities are defined as those activities which the teacher plans and prepares. The teacher is at the center of all action — motivating, presenting ideas, giving demonstrations, and directing the actions and interests of the children. Unstructured activities, on the other hand, may still be prepared by the teacher, but the children lead the action through self-directed play.

PROGRAM GOALS

Each center contains a unique group of children and adults. Each has its own geography and its children come from different segments of society. The goals and priorities of one program may differ from others. Common factors exist between centers. The following goals are acceptable to most programs. They give the assistant a basis for planning speech activities. Each child should be helped to attain these goals.

- Confidence in his own ability to use speech with others.
- Enjoyment of speaking experiences in play, conversations and groups.
- Acceptance of the idea that another's speech may be different.
- Interest in the meaning of new words.
- Using speech for his ideas, feelings and needs.

Fig. 10-1 Children speak and listen while they play.

- Using speech to solve problems.

- Using speech to create and for make-believe.

- Using speech and body actions at the same time.

- Waiting one's turn to speak.

The overall goal toward development of speech communication in the language arts is to increase each child's ability to use Standard English. Program goals can be realized primarily through (1) the planning of daily activities, (2) daily staff-child interaction, and (3) use of equipment and materials.

PLANNED PROGRAMS

A wide variety of different experiences provide learning opportunities. An activity can follow, review, and add depth to a previous one.

The special interests or needs of a group of children are included in planning daily programs. The programs then become more valuable and meaningful.

Fig. 10-2 Talking about the flower a child brought to school.

Some of the best activities happen when the teacher notices what the child or group is focusing on and uses the opportunity to expand interest, knowledge and enjoyment. A rainbow, a delivery truck or any chance happening can become the central topic of active speaking by the children, figure 10-2.

SETTINGS

Speaking activities occur inside, outside, and on the move. Preplanned activities are more successful when both children and teachers are comfortable, and distractions are blocked from view.

Close attention should be given to the seating space between children, and lighting and heating of the room; soft textures and rugs add warmth and comfort. A half circle with the teacher in the center provides a good view of both the teacher and what is to be seen.

Ease of viewing depends on eye level and seating arrangement. Whenever possible, the objects children are to look at should be at the child's eye level. Teachers often sit in child-sized chairs while conducting language arts experiences.

Screens, dividers and bookcases serve to cut down sights and sounds which distract the children's attention. Also, seating the children so they do not distract each other, before the activity starts, will give the activity a greater chance for success.

DAILY TEACHER-CHILD CONVERSATIONS

A child care assistant is a continual speech model for children. The following guides for assistant teachers in daily verbal conversations will be based on her understanding of the individual level of the child as preschoolers range in age and levels.

The following guidelines help develop speaking ability when dealing with young nonverbal or slightly verbal children.

Fig. 10-3 Let children see your face and mouth.

- Let them see your face and mouth clearly. Bend your knees, talk straight to them holding eye contact, figure 10-3.

- Use simple gestures and touch or show meanings with your hands as well as with your eyes as you talk, figure 10-4.

- If possible, let the child touch, feel, smell, taste and see whatever interests him as you talk in simple sentences.

- Watch for the nonverbal reactions; the child's face or body actions may show interest, fear or other things, figure 10-5. Supply words to fit the situation. "Here's the ball." "The dog will not hurt you." "Do you want a cracker?"

- Talk to the nonverbal child slowly, stressing key words such as nouns and verbs. Repeat them if he does not seem to understand.

- If you cannot understand his one word to you, repeat it back to him in a relaxed way. Say "Show me, Mary," if the child tries again and you still cannot understand her.

- Accept a child's try at a word. If he says "lellow," say, "Yes, the paint is yellow." His articulation will improve as he grows older and as he observes good speech models.

Fig. 10-4 "Eric, you can paint on this easel."

Fig. 10-5 A face can say a lot to a teacher.

- Answer expressive jargon or jabbering with suitable statements such as, "You're telling me." or "You don't say." Go along with his desire to put a string of words together. *Jargon* is defined as a group of sounds without recognizable words.

- Play games in which the child copies sounds or words; make games fun. Stop before he loses interest.

- Watch for his lead. If he is interested in some activity or object, talk about it in simple sentence statements. "The kitty feels soft." "Pet the kitty." or "Bobby's going down the slide.", figure 10-6.

- Make commands simple. "Time to go inside, now." Use gestures with the words. "Put the toys in the box." (Indicate actions as you say the words.)

- Reward the child's imitations (whether verbal or nonverbal) with smiles or touch or words. Show you appreciate his effort.

The following guidelines help develop speaking ability when dealing with the child who speaks in one word phrases or simple sentences.

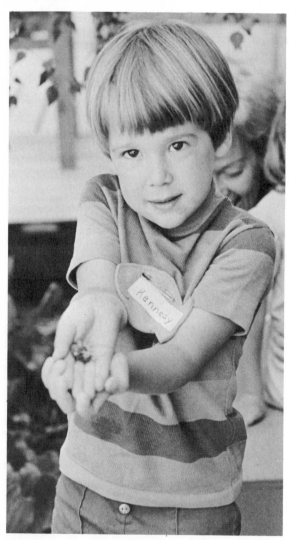

Fig. 10-6 If he is interested in some activity or object, talk about it with him.

- Enlarge his one word into meaningful simple sentences. "Ball" "Yes, it is a ball."

- Use the right words to describe objects and actions. "The *red* ball is *round*." "The dog wants to *lick* your *hand*."

- Use conjunctions (and, but, so, also, or) in your speech as well as possessives (mine, theirs, ours, Billy's, yours, his, hers) and negatives (is not, will not, do not, isn't, don't, won't, am not).

- Help the child talk about his feelings. "You are angry because he took your toy."

- Use old (already learned) words with new words. "The black *candy* is called *licorice*." "Your dog is a *poodle*, this dog is a *beagle*." "It's a kind of *hat* called a *baseball cap*."

- Ask simple questions which help the child to find out and discover while his interest is keen. "How does it feel?"

- Play labeling games with pictures, objects, etc.

- Correct speech errors, such as "wented" or "goed," by repeating *unobtrusively* (without calling attention to the correct form). "Yesterday, you *went* to the store." He may answer by saying it the same as before but you have modeled correct usage and in time he will copy it.

- Accept hesitant speech and stuttering in a relaxed, interested way. Putting words and ideas into words, when excited or under stress is difficult.

- Wait patiently while he tries; silently hold eye contact. He may lose the thought, but he will be back if you're a good listener, and if you respond with interest to what he has to say.

When the child speaks in sentences and comes close to mature speech, the teacher should

- Include appropriate classifications or categories in sentences to help children form concepts. "Dogs and cats are *animals*."

- Ask questions which help the child pinpoint the identifying characteristic. "How is the ball like the orange?"

- Ask questions that help the child to see what is alike and what is different.

- After modeling a sentence pattern in conversation, ask a simple question so the child can imitate the proper form while it is still fresh in his mind. "I think this lemon tastes sour." "How does the lemon taste to you?"

- Help the child keep ideas in step-by-step order. What happened first? What next? What came last?

- State commands clearly, building from one to two or three-part directions. "First wash your hands, then you can have a cracker."

- Use prepositions in your speech. Say them with gestures. "You put the toy *on* the shelf." "Thank you, the blocks go *inside* the box." (Use your hand to show position as you speak.)

- Use adjectives (big, little, bright, red, soft, etc.) and comparatives (more, less, lighter, heavier, shorter, tallest). "Tell me about the rubber doll." "Yes, this pink doll is bigger."

- Ask the child to carry simple verbal messages to another staff member. "Tell Mrs. Brown it's time to fix the snack." Alert other staff members to the fact that you are trying to promote verbal memory and self-confidence.

- Help the child discover causes and effects. "Teacher, I'm afraid of bugs." "Why do bugs make you afraid, Billy?"

- Remember that what you say in response to the child helps him in many ways. Really listen. Answer every child if possible. When the children talk at the same time, say "I want to hear each one." "Mary, say it again. John you can talk next."

QUESTIONING SKILLS

The teacher's questions often prompt children to think. Questions can also help children see details they would otherwise have missed. Sometimes questions help form relationships between objects and ideas; they may get children to speak about both feelings and thoughts; they can lead the child to a new interest.

Skill in questioning is an important teaching ability. Many times questions by their teacher may lead children to discovery.

Answering a question with a question depends upon the circumstances. When a child says "What does a rabbit eat?" the teacher might say "How could we find out?," knowing a real experience would be better than a quick answer.

When using questions, the level of difficulty should be recognized. Teachers try to help each child succeed in activities while offering a challenge at the same time.

Questions using *what* or *where* usually receive one-word or word-phrase answers.

Do you? Did you? Can you? Will you? Have you? Would you? questions can be answered by *yes* or *no*. This type of question fits the level of the very young.

Questions which help a child to think, compare or connect ideas may begin with:

What would happen if . . . ?
Which one is longer?
How are these two alike?

Why did you say these were different?

What happened next?

If it fell off the table, what would . . . ?

Can you guess which one will be first?

Where is the smallest one?

Could this ball fit inside this can?

The following are examples of questions which encourage problem solving or stimulate creative thought.

If you had a handful of pennies, what would you buy?

Tell me what you are going to do when you're big like your dad?

Can you think of a way to open this coconut?

How could we find out where this ant lives?

These questions can be answered by the more mature speakers.

By attentively listening and observing, the child care assistants may form questions which the child will want to answer.

SUMMARY

Each early childhood educational program is based on goals. Goals state the attitudes and abilities that a center wishes to develop in children. Planned activities and daily teacher-child conversations help the school reach its goals.

Teachers plan for both group and individual needs.

Questions are asked by both children and teachers. By observing, listening and interacting, teachers are better able to promote speaking abilities.

SUGGESTED ACTIVITIES

- Give five speaking area goals in your own order of priority.

- Interview a preschool teacher, or teachers. Get their reaction to the question, "If you could only do one thing to help young children's speaking ability, what would that be?"

- Observe a preschool group. What differences do you notice in the children's ability to solve problems with words? Cite specific examples.

REVIEW

A. Explain what is meant by the following:

1. structured activities
2. unobtrusively
3. possessives
4. negatives
5. prepositions
6. comparatives

B. 1. How can the goals of a program be met?

2. When children are interested in an object or happening, what should the assistant teacher do in order for the children to learn while motivation is present?

3. How can the environment around teacher-directed activities be made comfortable?

4. Where should visual materials be placed?

C. Select the correct answer or answers.

1. When a child says "wented",

    a. correct him.

    b. ignore him.

    c. unobtrusively repeat his message correctly.

    d. have him practice *went*.

2. In daily conversations, the teacher should

    a. answer or respond to nonverbal messages.

    b. pair new word meanings with words the child already knows.

    c. remain silent if a child yells at you in anger.

    d. accept stuttering and hesitant speech in a relaxed manner.

3. If a child says "Richlotti-gongo" to you,

    a. repeat it back if you can, hoping the child will show you what he means to communicate.

    b. ignore it and wait until you understand the message.

    c. go along with a statement saying something like "Really, you don't say."

    d. ask him to speak more clearly.

4. In using questions with young children,

    a. suit the question to the child.

    b. always give him the answer.

    c. insist that he answers correctly.

    d. answer some of the children's questions with your own when appropriate.

5. Activities are planned, based on

    a. goals only.

    b. children's current interests only.

    c. goals and children's interests.

    d. knowledge instead of attitudes.

D. Name three ways how an assistant teacher can give children confidence in their speaking abilities.

E. Select the appropriate teacher response to the children's comments.

Child	Teacher
1. "Dolly"	1. "Did the door hit you? And then what happened?"
2. "Where do this go?"	2. "Yes, they are. Is a dog as big as a cow?"
3. "I fell down. The door hit me."	3. "They taste good, you're right."
4. "Horses are big like cows."	4. "Where does the block go?" "The block goes on the top shelf."
5. "Dem er goodums."	5. "You can play with this dolly."
6. "That's a mouse, teacher."	6. It has fur like a mouse. It's small like a mouse, but it's called a hamster."

unit 11 climate and setting for speaking

OBJECTIVES

After studying this unit, the student should be able to

- Describe factors which would encourage development of speaking abilities.
- Explain the role of the child care assistant in dramatic play.
- Name activities or describe techniques which promote speaking.

A center should be a place full of interesting and active things to do with teachers and other children. Speech flows best when a child is relaxed rather than pressured or tense. There should be both a desire and a need to speak present, figure 11-1.

What makes a child use his speaking abilities in an early childhood center? There are many factors. Daily teacher-child conversation was discussed in an earlier unit, but there are others.

PLAY

Play itself produces much child-to-child conversation. Some types of play promote talking more than others. Quiet activities such as painting or working jigsaw puzzles may tend to limit speech communication somewhat while the child is deeply absorbed, figure 11-2. Teachers plan opportunities for children to play by themselves and with others in small and large groups. Play with another person or a small group almost always requires a child to speak. Very young children may play together without speaking in a nonverbal, imitative manner, but as they grow older they use more words. The interaction with other children offers increasing opportunity to grow in speaking ability.

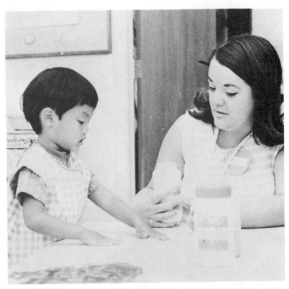

Fig. 11-1 There should be both a desire and a need to speak.

Fig. 11-2 Some activities tend to quiet speech while the child is absorbed in what he is doing.

DRAMATIC PLAY

Early in life children act out and repeat the words and actions of others. During preschool years this is often called *dramatic play,* and the staffs in early childhood centers plan and prepare for it. This type of play holds many learning opportunities. It helps the child to:

- Develop conversational skills and the ability to express his ideas in words.

- Understand the feelings, roles or work of others.

- Connect actions with words. Actions and words go hand-in-hand in dramatic play.

- Develop vocabulary.

- Develop creativity. The child imagines and acts, making things up as play goes on.

Fig. 11-3 Dramatic play promotes social interaction.

- Engage in social interaction with other children, figure 11-3.

- Cope with life sometimes through re-enactment of troubling situations by giving him an outlet for emotion. (Almost every doll in an early childhood center gets a spanking periodically when children play house.)

- Assume leadership and group participant roles.

"Let's pretend" is hardly ever a problem. When playing house, the child may start out as grandfather and end up as the baby or the family dog. Considerable time and effort is devoted to this type of play in childhood. The child works often and hard at it and has the ability to slide easily from the real world into make-believe.

As the child does not create from a vacuum, rich home and school experiences (going places and doing things) serve as building blocks for dramatic play. One would have a difficult time playing *restaurant* or *wedding* if there had been no previous experience with either.

Early childhood centers may provide activities that promote dramatic play.

- Field trips

- Visitors and guest speakers

- Books

- Pictures and discussions

- Films, filmstrips and slides

- Preparation of kits, equipment and settings for dramatic play

Dramatic Play Settings

A playhouse area with a child-sized stove, refrigerator, table and chairs encourage dramatic play. An old boat, a service station pump, and a telephone booth are other pieces of equipment that children enjoy using in their play.

Furniture normally found at early childhood centers, can be moved into room arrangements that suggest a bus, a house, a tunnel, or store. Large cardboard boxes become a variety of different props with, or without, word labels. Large paper bags, ropes, blankets and discarded work clothes or dress-up clothing also stimulate the child to pretend. Items for dramatic play may be obtained from shops, secondhand stores, flea market sales, garage sales, and other sources.

Dramatic Play Kits

Items that go together and suggest the same type of play can be boxed together ready for use. A shoeshine kit complete with cans of natural shoe polish, soft cloth, shoe brush, play money, a newspaper, or magazine is very popular. Other ideas for kits to be used in dramatic play are:

Post Office. Large index cards, stamp pads, stampers, crayon or pencils, stamps (i.e. Christmas seals), shoe box with slot cut in front and name clearly printed on.

Cleaning Set. Several brooms, mops, sponge mops, dust cloths, sponges and toweling for windows.

Tea Party. Set of cups, saucers, etc., plastic pitchers, napkins, vase, tablecloth, plastic spoons, small grocery containers like cereal boxes, etc.

Doctor. Stethoscope, medicine bottles, adhesive tape, cotton balls, plastic hypos, armband with a red cross on it, bag to carry.

Nurse. Same items as those for doctor kit, plus nurses caps. Caps can be made of cloth, or the bottom of the large size plastic bleach bottles may be used with a red cross mark on them.

Teacher. Notebooks, pencils, plastic glasses, chalk, book about the first day in Kindergarten.

Washing tiny babies. Large pieces of toweling to cover the table, several tiny dolls, some sets of toy bathroom furniture, individual plastic pitchers or bowls with soapy water (can be made from plastic bleach bottles), small pieces of toweling, cotton balls, individual talcum cans.

Supermarket. Cash register, play money, paper pads and pencils or crayons, punchers, paper sacks, empty food cartons, wax fruit.

Beauty Parlor. Plastic brushes, combs, cotton balls, powder, scarves, colored water in nail polish bottles, lip pomade.

Service Station. Tire pump, pliers, cans, sponges, and bucket; short length of hose and cylinder (for gas pump), hat, squirt bottle, paper towels, paper and pencil, sign "gas for sale."

Boat or Fisherman. Hats, bamboo lengths (about 3 feet) with string and magnet at the end, a basin, small metal objects such as paper clips for the fish. Fish shapes can also be cut out and a paper clip attached to each (for the magnet).

More kits can be made for the following games:

T.V. Repairman	*Birthday Party or Tea Party*
Picnic	
Car Wash	*Milkman*
Restaurant	*Spaceman*
Wedding	*Policeman*

Teacher's Role

Dramatic play is child directed instead of teacher directed; it comes from the child's imagination, with actions to accompany his thoughts.

The child care assistant remains in the background. She is watchful and sometimes suggests a new direction, but then removes herself so the flow of play is decided by the children. Her close presence, or words, can stop and change behavior when the safety of the situation gets out of hand; otherwise the ideas, words and dramatic play actions are those of the children.

DAILY ROUTINES

Early childhood centers include periods for talking in their programs. Roll call at the start of the day is used to encourage speaking. Snack and lunch periods are set up to promote pleasant conversation while eating, figure 11-4.

Activities are planned and structured to provide for as much child talk as possible. One of the most common pastimes is "Show and Tell." This game encourages children to talk about their special interests in front of others. Most often the child brings something from home or shares something made or accomplished at school. Some helpful hints for conducting "Show and Tell" are:

- Encourage, don't force the child to speak. If he doesn't want to talk, have him just show.

- Let the child stand or sit near the teacher.

- Stimulate the other children to ask the child questions.

- Limit time of the overtalkative child by using an egg timer.

Fig. 11-4 Snack times may be talking times.

- Be careful the activity does not last too long or the children become bored.

- Thank each child for his participation.

- Try something new such as:

  a. displaying all articles and having the group guess who brought what.

  b. having children swap what they have brought so they talk about each other's items.

  c. bringing in some teacher surprise items to share.

  d. making a caption for each item and displaying it on a table (Betty's Green Rock.)

  e. having the child hide the object behind his back while describing it to the others and having them guess what it is.

Show-and-tell items are usually kept out of reach to prevent the loss of a valued or favorite toy. Occasionally, mothers complain that the child feels it is necessary to bring an item every day. Some schools have boy days, girl days, or turn days. The purpose of show and tell is to promote vocabulary development, responsibility, and speaking in front of others. It is helpful to make this purpose known to parents.

LEADING ACTIVITIES

A child can be chosen to lead others in activities if he is familiar with the routines and activities. A child can alert the others by saying the right words or calling out the names of the children who need a cup or a cookie. One or more children can be in front leading songs or finger plays (finger plays will be discussed in the next unit). There are many times when individual children can be chosen as the speaker, or speakers to direct routines with words.

Directions such as "Billy, will you pass the wastebasket, please" and "If you're through, throw your cup away" may capture his interest and give him a speaking opportunity.

A watchful child care assistant encourages the children to speak in many ways. The child tends to speak more if his speech is given attention and rewarded with a smile and an answer. It is helpful during group times, to point out that the teacher and the other children want to hear what everyone says and, because of this, children should take turns in speaking.

SUMMARY

When there is a relaxed atmosphere with interested teachers and sufficient activity, more talking takes place. Playing with others helps vocabulary development and language acquisition in settings where children interact with reality and make-believe. The teacher's role in dramatic play is to set the stage but remain in the background so the children can do it on their own.

Dramatic play settings and kits are available, and are boxed and collected by the child care assistants.

Part of a child care assistant's work is to encourage children to talk, to give children opportunities to lead speaking activities and to ensure that children are "talked with" and not "talked at."

SUGGESTED ACTIVITIES

- Visit a center and record all instances of dramatic play. Note all equipment that seems to promote speaking.

- With a classmate, select one of the dramatic play kit ideas which did not suggest items to be found in the kit. List the items you feel would be safe and promote dramatic play on that theme.

- Role play "playing house" with some classmates: assign mother, father, brother, sister, baby, family dog, and grandmother, or other family roles.
    Pretend you are having breakfast or dinner; traveling in the car going on vacation; or are in other family situations, such as father or mother breaking the news to the family about a raise in pay or new job. Try a bedtime situation. Were there any instances of one or more family members coping with life through the enactment? If not, have the group discuss how young children might possibly have done so in the same role-playing situation.

- Conduct a "Show and Tell" time with a group of young children.

- Observe a full morning program in a center. List the activities or routines in which there was active speaking by most of the children.

REVIEW

A. Define:

1. Dramatic play

2. Coping

3. Routines

B. Select the correct responses:

1. Some of the factors which might help young children develop speaking abilities are:

    a. equipment

    b. staff members

    c. parents

    d. making a child ask correctly for what he wants

    e. a relaxed atmosphere

    f. interesting happenings to talk about

    g. lack of play with other children

    h. asking a child to recite

    i. a need or desire on the child's part

    j. a teacher's ignoring the child's nonverbal communication

    k. daily speaking routines

    l. teacher attention to speech

    m. teacher rewarding children's speech

    n. planned speaking activities

C. Answer the following questions

1. Describe what is meant by a dramatic play kit.

2. Name some of the things a child care assistant does *not* want to happen during show-and-tell time?

    (Example)   One child talking too long.

D. Select the terms that best define the teacher's role in dramatic play.

1. an interactor

2. a background observer

3. a provider of settings

4. a provider of props

5. a redirector of unsafe play

6. an active participant

7. a suggestor of ideas during play

8. a provider of many words

9. a gatherer of dramatic play items

E. Name three occupational dramatic play kits.

F. In the following description of calling the role, identify those parts that might make a child feel pressured and tense rather than relaxed. Discuss the attitude of the teacher as well.

> "Good morning children. Everyone say Good Morning, Mrs. Brown. That's good. Bonnie, you didn't say it, you were playing with your hair ribbon. Say it now, Bonnie.
>
> I'm going to say everyone's name. When I say your name I want you all to say, 'I'm here Mrs. Brown.' Susie Smith. 'I'm here Mrs. Brown.' Speak louder Susie, we can't hear you. Brett Porter. Not 'I'm present Brett,' say 'I'm here Mrs. Brown.' David Martinez. David Martinez. Answer please, David. David Martinez. David, you must answer when I call your name! Andy Smith. No, Andy, say 'I'm here Mrs. Brown,' not 'I'm here' and that's all.
>
> I don't know what's the matter with all of you; you did it right yesterday. We're going to stay here until we all do it the right way. Dana Collins. I can't understand what you said Dana, say it again. Mark Jefferson. Mark, that's very good, you said it the right way. Chris Peters. No it's not time to talk to Ronnie now, it's time to speak up. What are you supposed to say, children? I give up, you'll never learn. Let's all go outside now and work out all of our wiggles."

unit 12 speaking activities

OBJECTIVES

After studying this unit, the student should be able to

- Describe a variety of speaking activities.
- Perform a finger play with children.
- Discuss ways to promote child involvement in simple plays.

Activities in this unit give the child many speaking opportunities. The child will talk about most early childhood experiences – if they are interesting. It is difficult to sort activities into listening activities and speaking activities as they often go hand-in-hand. The activities found in this unit provide the opportunity to imitate speech, to use creative speech, and for the child to express his own ideas and feelings.

FINGER PLAY

Children usually enjoy finger play very much. Parents have probably introduced this type of play early in life with "peek-a-boo" or "this little piggy went to market." Finger plays use words and actions (usually finger motions) together. Early childhood play goes

Fig. 12-1 Finger plays use words and action together.

beyond finger movements and often include whole body actions, figure 12-1.

When learning a finger play, the child usually practices and joins in the finger movements before he learns or adds the words. Words may be learned and retained by doing the play over and over again.

Finger plays are often done in rhyme, but need not be. Rhymes, being easier to remember, give the child ear pleasure, and a chance to feel good about himself. First, the child quickly becomes one of a group having fun and doing the same thing. Secondly, he experiences a feeling of self-worth when he has learned a rhyme.

Child care assistants use finger plays at any time of the day for speech development; to get the "wiggles" out; to keep children active and interested while waiting; or between activities. They are also useful for special purposes, such as quieting a group, or getting toys back on the shelves.

Finger plays can build vocabulary as well as teach children facts. They can also help a child release pent-up energy.

Teachers should practice a finger play, memorizing it beforehand for a clear and smooth presentation. It should be offered enthusiastically, focusing on enjoyment. As with other activities, the teacher can say "Try it with me" or "Let's see if you can do it too." The child who just watches will join in when ready. Watching comes first, one or two hand movements next, and, after repetitions, both words and actions together. Each child learns at his own rate of speed, figure 12-2.

Finger plays appeal to the imagination of the young child and keep him active using both words and motions. They also help him to feel good about himself for he quickly learns to do what the teacher and others are doing and enjoying.

SUGGESTED FINGER PLAYS

Finger plays can be found in many books for early childhood staff members, or be self-created. The following are suggested because of their popularity with both children and teachers.

HICKORY, DICKORY, DOCK

Hickory, dickory, dock!
 (rest elbow in the palm of the other hand
 and swing upraised arm back and forth)
The mouse ran up the clock;
 (creep fingers up the arm to the palm of
 the other hand)
The clock struck one,
 (clap hands)
The mouse ran down.
 (creep fingers down to elbow)
Hickory, dickory, dock!
 (swing arm as before)

OPEN, SHUT THEM

Open, shut them. Open, shut them.
Give a little clap.
Open, shut them. Open, shut them.
Lay them in your lap.

Creep them, creep them,
Creep them, creep them,
Right up to your chin.
Open wide your little mouth
But do not let them in.

Open, shut them. Open, shut them,
To your shoulder fly
Let them, like the little birdies
Flutter to the sky.

Falling, falling, downward falling
Almost to the ground,
Quickly raising all your fingers
Twirl them 'round and 'round and 'round.

CHOO!! CHOO!!

Choo-o! Choo-o! Choo! Choo!
 (run finger along arm to shoulder slowly)
This little train goes up the track.

Choo! Choo! Choo! Choo!
 (at shoulder turn "train" and head down arm)
But this little train comes quickly back.
Choo-choo-choo-choo! choo-choo-choo-choo!

 (repeat last line)
 (run fingers down arm quickly)
Whoo-o! Whoo-o! Whoo-o!
 (imitate train whistle)

TWO LITTLE BLACKBIRDS

Two little blackbirds sitting on a hill,
 (place 2 forefingers on shoulders to represent birds
One named Jack,
 (hold one forefinger out)
One named Jill.
 (hold other forefinger out)
Fly away Jack; Fly away Jill;
 (make one hand and then other "fly away")
Come back Jack; Come back Jill.
 (bring hands back to shoulders one at a time)

SLEEPY TIME

Open wide your little hands,
Now squeeze them very tight.
Shake them, shake them very loose,
With all your might.
Climb them slowly to the sky,
Drop down like gentle rain.
Go to sleep my little hands,
I'll waken you again.
(stop here if the play is used to quiet children)

Fig. 12-2 Each child learns finger play at his own rate of speed.

Sleepy time is over now,
Wake up each little hand.
You've been quiet as a mouse,
Now play you're in a band.
Clappety-clappety-clappety clap,
We're having lots of fun.
Clappety-clappety-clappety clap.
Stop! Little hands, you're done.

A FUNNY ONE

'Round the house
'Round the house
    (fingers around face)
Peep in the window
    (open eyes wide)
Listen at the door
    (cup hand behind ear)
Knock at the door
    (knock on head)
Lift up the latch
    (push up nose)
And walk in
    (stick out tongue and walk fingers in mouth)
— I caught you! (Bite gently down on fingers!)

TWO LITTLE APPLES

Two little apples hanging on a tree (hand by eyes)
Two little apples smiling at me (smile)
I shook that tree as hard as I could (shake tree)
Down came the apples (make falling motions)
Mmm — they were good (rub stomach)

HALLOWEEN

Five little pumpkins sitting on a gate
    (hold up 5 fingers)
This one says, "My it's getting late"
    (wiggle index finger)
This one says, "There are black cats everywhere"
    (wiggle middle finger)
This one says, "I don't care."
    (wiggle ring finger)
This one says, "It's all for Halloween fun"
    (wiggle little finger)
And the other one says, "We better run"
    (wiggle thumb)
Wooo, goes the wind (blow)
Out goes the light! (close eyes)
And the 5 little pumpkins run quickly out of sight.
    (hand runs away)

TOUCH YOUR NOSE[1]

Touch your nose,
Touch your chin,
That's the way this game begins.
Touch your eyes,
Touch your knees,
Now pretend you're going to sneeze.
    (finger under nose)

Touch your hair,
Touch one ear,
Touch your two red lips right here.
Touch your elbows
Where they bend,
That's the way this touch game ends.

PAT-A-CAKE

Pat-a-cake, pat-a-cake, baker's man
Bake me a cake (clap hands together lightly)
As fast as you can.
Roll it (pass hands over each other in circular motion)
And pat it (touch hands together lightly)
And mark it with "B" (write "B" with index finger)
And toss it in the oven for baby and me.
    (Stretch out arms as if putting cake in oven)

BEEHIVE

Here is a beehive (make fist around other hand)
Where are the bees?
Hidden away
Where nobody sees.

See them creeping (pull out one finger at a time)
Out of the hive
1-2-3-4-5! Buzz! (make buzzing sound with hand
        moving in the air)

Here is a beehive (make fist)
Where are the bees!
They're buzzing around (buzz around with other hand)
The flowers and trees.

Soon they'll come home
Back from their fun (put thumb in first then fingers
            one at a time)
5-4-3-2-1! Buzz! (make buzzing sound)

[1]Louise Binder Scott and J.J. Thompson, <u>Rhymes for Fingers</u> <u>and Flannelboards</u> (New York: McGraw Hill Inc.)

BODY ACTION PLAYS

TEDDY BEAR, TEDDY BEAR

Encourage child to jump in rhythm to this jumprope chant while doing what rhyme says, if you use this for working out the wiggles.

Teddy bear, teddy bear, turn around,
Teddy bear, teddy bear, touch the ground,
Teddy bear, teddy bear, show your shoe,
Teddy bear, teddy bear, that will do.

Teddy bear, teddy bear, go upstairs (alternate hands
*   upwards)*
Teddy bear, teddy bear, say your prayers.
Teddy bear, teddy bear, turn off the light,
Teddy bear, teddy bear, say goodnight. (lay down
*   pretend to snore)*

HEAD, SHOULDERS

Head, shoulders, knees and toes (stand with both
*   hands, touch in order)*
Head, shoulders, knees and toes
Head, shoulders, knees and toes
That's the way the story goes. (clap this line)
This is my head, this is not (hands on head then feet)
These are my shoulders, this is not (hands on shoulders,
*   then knees)*
Here are my knees, watch them wiggle, (wiggle knees)
Touch my armpits and I giggle. (hands under armpits
*   with laugh)*
Head, shoulders, knees and toes (touch in order)
That's the way the story goes. (clap)

RING AROUND THE ROSY

Ring around the rosy (form circle by holding hands)
Pockets full of posies (pretend to put something in
*   pocket)*
Ashes, Ashes,
All Fall down. (fall down)

Ring around the chair (place a chair in center of room,
*   form circle by holding hands)*
There's no one sitting there
Ashes, Ashes
All fall down.

Pick up all the toys (pick up a toy yourself)
Pick up all the toys
Put them all away, helpful girls and boys (put on shelf)

Ring around the rosy (form circle)
Pockets full of posies (pretend)
Ashes, Ashes
All fall down. (fall down)

Fig. 12-3 Young children watching a
puppet performance.

PUPPETS

Activities with hand puppets are one of the best known ways to produce speech. Children benefit by seeing teachers or others perform. Puppets can either be made or purchased, (see appendix), figure 12-3.

A cardboard box or a rope across a doorway can be used as a puppet theatre, (see appendix for additional ideas). If puppets are hung invitingly within view, they are likely to be used more often. Planned activities with puppets increase interest. The child is more apt to play with puppets if the child care assistant uses them to introduce activities and stories. She could place one on each hand and have the puppets speak to each other.

PLAY ACTING

Children can act out parts from favorite stories as well as scenes from real life. A child care assistant sets the stage for this activity, keeping the following points in mind:

- The child needs to be familiar with the story in order to know what happens first, next and last.

- Activities in which the child pretends to do an action, to be an animal, or to copy the actions of another, help prepare him for simple drama, figure 12-4.

- A first step would be to act without words or to the accompaniment of a good story, record or music.

- The teacher can be the narrator while the children are the actors.

- Children should be encouraged to volunteer for parts.

- Props or settings may be simple. Ask, "What could we use for a bridge?" or a similar question so children can use their creativity.

- The teacher should accept any imaginative acts, whether or not they are a part of the original story. She remains close, without directing or interfering (except when necessary).

- Individual and group actions should be praised and encouraged. Children should have turns playing the parts.

Some classic stories which lend themselves to puppet play are:

Fig. 12-4 Copying the actions of another helps prepare children for simple drama.

The Three Billy Goats Gruff
Goldilocks and the Three Bears
The Three Little Pigs
The Little Red Hen
Gingerbread Boy
Little Red Ridinghood

Fast action and simple story lines are best for the young child. Play acting presents many developmental opportunities:

- self-expression

- use of correct speech

- coordination of actions and words

- creative thinking

- self-confidence

- listening

- social interaction

PICTURE FILES

Pictures and photographs are used to motivate speech. Children can discuss what they see in the picture or photograph. Staff members of early childhood centers are usually collectors of pictures, photos and other illustrations. Magazine pictures that are colorful or stimulating and of interest to children are mounted on cardboard or construction paper. Simple word captions are sometimes added, as well as thought-provoking questions. Pictures of food, animals, transportation, flowers, sports, etc. can be collected and filed under these headings.

ANOTHER SPEAKING ACTIVITY

The Mystery Bag. An activity children enjoy in small groups is called the mystery bag. The teacher collects a series of common objects. Behind her back, she puts one of the objects in another bag. The game starts with a child reaching in the second bag; he describes the object, but does not look at it. It is then pulled out of the bag and discussed. "What can we do with it? What is it called? It's the same color as what else in the room?" The group should be small as it is hard for a small child to wait for a turn. Examples of objects which could be used are a rock, comb, orange, pancake turner, feather, plastic cup, sponge, hole punch, flower, toy animal, whistle.

CHILDREN'S FLANNELBOARD SETS

The use of flannelboard pieces such as felt and pellon can bring about the child's imitation of a favorite story or his creation of a new one. A large box with felt glued in the lid can be used for both storage and play.

GUESSING GAMES

Activities that ask for word responses give the child a reason to speak, and can be played as a game.

Parts of the Body Talking Time:

I can see you with my _____ ?   (eyes)

I can smell you with my _____ ?   (nose)

I can chew with my _____ ?   (teeth)

I can hear with my _____ ?   (ears)

I clap with my _____ ?   (hands)

I walk on my _____ ?   (feet)

I put food in my _____ ?   (mouth)

This is not my nose, it's my _____   (ears)
    (point to ears)

This is not my eye, it's my _____   (nose)
    (point to nose)

This is not my mouth, it's my _____   (eye)
    (point to eye)

GUESSING PICTURE MESSAGES

Duplicate the drawings shown here on large newsprint, figure 12-5. Help the children translate the messages into words.

Fig. 12-5 Guessing picture messages.

Reprinted with permission of the publishers, Allen Raymond, Inc. Darien, Conn. 06820, <u>EARLY YEARS</u> Magazine, January, 1973.

SUMMARY

Speaking activities are planned for the young child. Some require simple imitation of words while others call for the child's creative or expressive response.

Finger plays use words and actions together. They are actively enjoyed and build feelings of self-worth. Teachers memorize finger plays and use them daily.

Play acting is another worthwhile speaking activity in which the teacher sets the stage. Puppets are an invitation to speak, and many types are found at early childhood centers. Seeing and taking part in puppetry helps promote play and exploration. Picture and photographs can be mounted and filed for activities which promote speaking.

SUGGESTED ACTIVITIES

- With a small group of classmates, practice and present a finger play or body action play. Have each student present the finger play until it is learned by the others.

- Make a list of at least five books which are resources for finger plays.

- Present a finger play to a group of young children.

- Find a finger play that is seasonal and is generally used only at one time of year. Bring a copy to class.

- Ask a person involved in drama work for children to speak to the class.

- Find a simple play you feel young children might enjoy. Bring a copy to class.

- Collect ten pictures, photos, or illustrations. Mount them and write a series of questions on the back of each. Ask questions which require more than a one-word answer.

- Plan an activity in which children will be speaking. Describe: (1) Materials needed, (2) Getting started, (3) What happens next, and (4) What speaking abilities will be used.

- Bring a puppet to class. With a group of classmates, create, practice and present a puppet activity to another small group of classmates.

- Create a finger play for young children.

REVIEW

A. Sort the following into the best category describing the activity. The categories are Imitating Speech, Creating with Speech and Expressing Ideas with Speech.

finger plays	songs	body action chants
picture collections	acting out plays	child flannelboard sets
child using a puppet	mystery bag	daily conversations

B. Why are finger plays popular with young children?

C. Rearrange and place in the best order of sequence.

1. Child knows words and actions of a finger play.
2. Teacher knows words and actions of a finger play.
3. Teacher practices finger play.
4. Child participates with actions only.
5. Child watches.
6. Teacher presents finger play to children.
7. Teacher evaluates the results of the finger play.
8. Teacher encourages children to join in actions and words.

unit 13 understanding differences

OBJECTIVES

After studying this unit, the student should be able to

- Describe the assistant's role with children who speak with a dialect.
- Discuss the problems early childhood centers face with bilingual children.
- Identify common speaking difficulties and the teacher techniques which help young children.

Standard English is the language of elementary schools and textbooks. It is the language of the majority of Americans. Unfortunately for those who speak in a dialect, others may think of them as different. At times, this can be an advantage? more often, however, it is a disadvantage.

Dialect can be defined as a variation of language distinguished by vocabulary, grammar, and pronunciation that differs from Standard English and is spoken by a distinct group of people in a geographic location. A child may say, "You sound funny!" when meeting another child from a different part of our country. The other child answers, "You sound funny too."

Many regions of the country have dialectic differences. However, linguistic differences may occur anywhere. For example, some parts of the South may use "you-all"; yet, Spanish or black English may be the primary language in many parts of the country. Following are some examples of these differences. It must be emphasized that not all inhabitants of these areas speak in the manner indicated; much depends on environment, experiences and education.

STANDARD ENGLISH

"Sit over there."

"Fill up this bag."

"He is working."

"I happily remember
my early years."

"During the rainy season,
many people stay at home."

"I'm going home."

"He's doing nothing."

"Those."

"Jim likes candy."

DIALECTAL ENGLISH
Parts of the South

"You-all set yonder"

Parts of the West

"Fill up this sack."

Appalchia

"He's a-workin."

Another Primary language

"I remind with much happiness my
early years."

"In the rain-season, many people
don't get out from
their home."

"I'ma goin' home."

"He be doin nofin."

"Dose."

"Jim like candy."

In some areas where a language other than English is spoken, part of the rules of the second language may blend and combine to form a type of English, different from Standard. Two examples of this are English spoken by some Indian children, and English spoken in communities close to the Mexican border.

CHILD CARE ASSISTANT'S ROLE

Dialectic differences are of concern to the child care assistant. In order to give young children the best model possible, the teacher

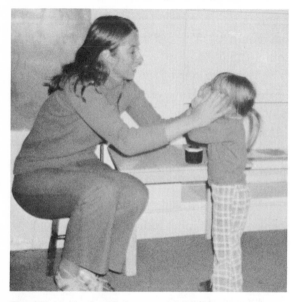

Fig. 13-1 A teacher's speech model is important.

Fig. 13-2 Teachers promote natural speech.

should speak Standard English. It matters very little to the child if the teacher speaks a bit differently than he speaks. However, the teacher's attitude, her warmth, and her acceptance of the dialect and the child himself is extremely important to the child, figure 13-1.

Staff members working with the young child respect the child's natural speech and do not try to stop the child from using it. A child may be a very good speaker of his particular dialect, or he may be just a beginner. The goal is the child's use of natural speech in his native dialect, figure 13-2.

The child's ability to pick up new words and new ways is at its peak during early years. Standard English can be taught by having many good speaking models available at the center for the children to hear. Interested adults, play activities, other children, and a rich language arts program will provide a setting where children listen and talk freely.

The child care assistant should know what parts of the center's program are designed to increase the children's use of words. The assistant teacher shows a genuine interest in words in her daily conversations with the children. She also uses the correct forms of Standard English in a casual way. Correcting the child in an obvious way could embarrass him and stop openness and enthusiasm. Careful listening, skillful responding, and appropriate questioning during conversations, will help the child learn to put his thoughts into words. He thinks in terms of his own dialect first, and in time, will express them in Standard English.

BILINGUALISM

Many centers deal with children who speak another language, or very little English. A center with bilingual children has many decisions to make. The first concern should be the child's adjustment to school. Every effort is made to make the child feel at ease before attempts are made to teach him a second language. Often, the teacher or assistant is bilingual (speaks both languages).

Recent studies of children who speak two languages point out that it is more important that the child learn the second language during his early years and that both the first and second language are learned well during this period. In the past many teachers felt that having another language well developed before the first grade would tend to confuse and defeat the child. This occurs if the school expects too much, too soon. Reading becomes more difficult for the child, if the school has not had a well-developed program in speaking and understanding English vocabulary before reading is begun. Teachers who teach English as a second language need training and a knowledge of the differences between the two languages in grammar, speech sounds, and sentence structure. They also need an understanding of the customs of the area, figure 13-3.

The child care assistant should have knowledge of the program the school has planned for each child, particularly when bilingual children attend. A variety of plans and methods to help the bilingual child exist in early childhood centers.

Bilingualism need not be a disadvantage — it can be an advantage. Proper staff attitude and ability to hold the child's interest and build his self-confidence while teaching him English is a challenge and reward, figure 13-4.

DISADVANTAGED LANGUAGE OPPORTUNITY

The word *disadvantaged* to many simply means being poor. A child who lacks opportunities and the essentials needed for growth and development comes to an early childhood center with less language. Lack of money in the home may be but one factor. Poverty takes its toll on a family's spirit and energy.

However, many poor homes are rich in love, strength and sacrifice, and the type of home life needed for the growth and development of language; others, unfortunately, are not.

Much has been written and researched concerning the differences in the language development of the child in the middle and the lower social class. A child from a different background may come to school with some disadvantages:

- a smaller vocabulary, using more gestures and single words

Fig. 13-3 Teachers understand that what is familiar in one child's culture may not be familiar or of interest to a child with a different cultural background.

Fig. 13-4 Staff attitude can build each child's feeling's of self-confidence.

- fewer skills in problem-solving with language; that is, labeling, classifying, generalizing and ability to see cause and effect relationships

- a less developed listening ability, and less ability to gather and process information through sensory organs

- less familiarity with middle-class modes of expression

Fortunately, not all young children from disadvantaged homes have all the symptoms mentioned. Also, the child may have other positive personality strengths, such as independence, that are often overlooked. The life experiences of these disadvantaged children are of a different nature than the life experiences of the middle class child; therefore they will have different interests. Programs that are meaningful start with activities of interest. Child care assistants need to know the children's life styles in order to plan and interact appropriately. A planned, well-understood program by the staff is absolutely necessary.

Most program plans emphasize the following activities:

Fig. 13-5 Teachers try to spend as much time with quiet children as they spend with talkative ones.

- Activities which develop sensory skills
  . . visual, auditory, and tactile (touch)
  . . discriminatory, relational, and sequential abilities

- Activities which promote problem solving and concept development
  . . classifying, organizing and associating

- Activities which deal with the language arts, and vocabulary and comprehension development
  . . listening, speaking, printscript and symbolic forms

Programs are developmental, starting with basics and moving toward higher levels. Supporting, rewarding and giving language feedback, which expands and clarifies what the child says as he plays, is the role of the child care assistant. This includes being an alert listener really hearing *what* children say more than *how* they say it. Good listeners can answer with logical statements and sincere interest. They can ask the child to tell more and to give details. They can suggest ideas or plans for the child to think about related to what he said. Not only does a child care assistant like children, she also likes to talk with them in a way that helps them grow in understanding and ability. She divides her time as equally as possible between the quiet children and the talkative ones, figure 13-5.

COMMON SPEECH ERRORS

As children learn to speak, they make many errors. Imperfections appear because (1) a child does not hear as well an adult, especially certain high-frequency consonant sounds. The child may not be able to distinguish sounds; they tend to sound the same, and (2) a child's coordination and control of his articulatory mechanisms may not be perfected. For example, he may be able to hear the difference between *Sue* and *shoe* but is not able to pronounce them differently.

Some of the errors young children make are listed for the assistant teacher's understanding.

Substitutions: One sound is substituted for another.
"Wabbit" for *rabbit*
"Git" for *get*

Omissions: The speaker leaves out a sound that should be articulated. He says "ca" for *cat,* "icky" for *sticky,* "probly" for *probably.* The left-out sound may be at the beginning, middle or end of a word.

Distortions: Production of a sound in an inarticulate manner.

Additions: The speaker adds a sound. "Li-it-tle" for *little.* "Muv-va-ver" for *mother.*

Transposition: Sounds of a word are switched in position.
"Hangerber" for *hamburger*
"Modren" for *modern*

Lisps: A distortion of *s, z, sh, zh, ch* and *j* sounds. There are from 2 to 10 types of lisps noted by speech authorities.

Stuttering: A repetition of sounds, usually at the beginning of the word.

All or some of the preceding errors may be found in the speech of young children. Although most will disappear with time and access to good speech models, some may persist and need speech therapy and correction. A child care assistant can alert the director to observe children she feels could benefit from professional help.

SUMMARY

Child care assistants may work with children who differ greatly in language development because of speech difficulties.

The role of the child care assistant is to carefully work toward increasing the child's use of words while providing a model of Standard English through activities and daily interaction.

Program goals should be clearly understood, as should the needs and interests of children who have developed a language which differs from the language of the school. Cultural differences exist, and teachers need to be aware of them in order to understand the young child. Knowing cultural differences helps the assistant to provide activities which start at the child's present level, and helps the child to grow, know more, speak more, and speak in Standard English.

SUGGESTED ACTIVITIES

- List and describe dialects found in your community. Give a few sentence examples of each.

- In small groups, discuss what you feel are essential factors to language growth that may be missing in a poverty child's background.

- Interview the director of a center which cares for bilingual and/or disadvantaged young children. Ask what techniques are used to increase a child's language ability. If a center does not exist in your community, give examples of goals or techniques used to increase a child's language ability which you have found from research at a library.

- Ask a speech therapist or a specialist in speech correction to speak to your class.

- Observe three preschool children (one at a time) for a period of 10 minutes each. Write down exactly what each child says. Include a description of gestures and nonverbal communications. Analyze your notes. Are there any examples of common speech errors or dialect differences?

- Compare two languages. What are the differences? The similarities?

REVIEW

A. Answer the questions.

1. How can a child care assistant learn about the cultural background of a child?

2. What should be the teacher's attitude toward children who have a speech that is different from the teacher's?

3. How can teachers learn about ways that a child's first language might differ from English?

4. One of the responsibilities of a child care assistant is to act as a model to the child for correct forms of speech. Another responsibility is to increase the child's ability to express his ideas in words. Quality of responses is more important than just talking. In the following exchange between teachers and small children, why did the child stop speaking?

    a. Teacher: "How are you today Mary?"

       Child: "Fine."

    b. Child: "Mrs. Brown, Johnny hit me!"

       Teacher: "I saw you grab the truck he was playing with, that wasn't nice!"

       Child: (Silence)

    c. Child: "Teacher, I want a crayon."

       Teacher: "Do you know how to use a crayon?"

       Child: "Yes."

       Teacher: "Tell me how you use a crayon."

       Child: "To color."

       Teacher: "Say to make colored marks on the paper."

       Child: "I want a crayon."

       Teacher: "How are you going to use the crayon?"

       Child: (Silence)

     d. Child: "Fellow one."

        Teacher: "It's yellow not fellow."

        Child: "Fellow one."

        Teacher: "You want the yellow one. A fellow is a man, Lindy."

        Child: (Silence)

     e. Child: "I found a bug."

        Teacher: "That's nice."

     f. Teacher: "Jason, what's your favorite ice cream flavor?"

        Child: "Huh?"

        Teacher: "What's your favorite ice cream flavor?"

        Child: "Flavorite?"

        Teacher: "Don't you like ice cream?"

        Child: "Yah."

        Teacher: "What's your favorite ice cream flavor?"

        Child: (Silence)

B.   Define these speech terms.

    1. dialect   4. transposition
    2. bilingual   5. disadvantage
    3. stuttering   6. lisp

C.   Listed below are comments made by children. Give an example of the response which a child care assistant teacher could make in order to encourage more thought and stimulate growth on the part of the child.

    1. Child with ball says, "Me play."

    2. Child remarks, "I done went to get a red crayon."

    3. Child says, "I got this thing."

    4. Child says, "I like chitchun choop!"

    5. Child asks, "No run in the street?"

    6. Child exclaims, "I don't wanna play with them childruns."

D.   Select the numbered phrase which best describes the lettered items.

    1. a dialect

    2. a common speech error

3. a teacher technique

   a. Modeling

   b. "Chocklit canny"

   c. Increasing native speech

   d. Southern drawl

   e. "I've this idear"

   f. Western twang

   g. Casual correction

   h. "Hangerber"

   i. "Get that hoss over cheer"

   j. "Muddah and Faddah"

   k. Asking questions for problem solving with words

   l. Extending conversations

   m. Interesting activities

   n. "Peter Wabbit"

   o. Planning sensory activities

   p. "I'm sittin' here"

   q. "I don't got none"

   r. "I chur like ya"

   s. "Thip the thoop"

   t. Promoting inquiry

E. Select *all* correct answers to each numbered item.

   1. Standard English is

      a. the language of textbooks.

      b. what all teachers should model.

      c. often different from English spoken in a dialect.

      d. needed for success in any line of work.

   2. Early childhood centers try to

      a. teach children Standard English during the first days at school.

      b. make sure each child feels secure.

      c. plan activities in which disadvantaged children have interest.

      d. provide for each child's development of use of words in his own dialect.

3. Child care assistants should be careful to guard against

   a. casually correcting children's speech.

   b. an attitude within themselves which says Standard English is correct, therefore better than English spoken in a dialect.

   c. giving children the idea that they speak differently or "funny."

   d. feeling children who come from low-income homes are always disadvantaged when compared to children from middle-income homes.

4. Young children with speech errors

   a. rarely outgrow them.

   b. may need special help.

   c. often do not hear as well as adults.

   d. can hear that what they say is different but do not have the ability to say it correctly.

5. Bilingualism in the young child is

   a. always a disadvantage.

   b. sometimes a disadvantage.

   c. a rewarding challenge to the teacher.

   d. a problem when schools make children feel defeated and unaccepted.

6. A disadvantaged child

   a. may also be hyperactive and aggressive.

   b. may be more independent and talkative than a middle class child.

   c. may talk a lot but have a smaller vocabulary than the average middle class child.

   d. needs teachers who not only model Standard English but also model problem solving with words.

Section 4 Written Communication

unit 14 printscript

OBJECTIVES

After studying this unit the student should be able to

- Discuss the child's development of small hand muscle control.
- State three reasons why young children may start making alphabet letters or numerals.
- Describe how printscript upper and lowercase letters are formed.

A child will one day learn that written marks mean something. Just as he sought the name of everything, he now seeks both the names of these marks and what they say. As each child is individual, this may or may not happen during the preschool years. One child may try to make letters or numbers. Another child may have little interest or knowledge of written forms, figure 14-1. Most children will be somewhere in between these two examples.

Providing experiences which match a child's interest and ability is the goal of many centers. Most schools plan activities with alphabet letters for those children who ask questions or seem ready, and then proceed if the child is interested.

Fig. 14-1 Some children are interested in alphabet letters, others are not.

Patting the child on the head, and telling him he will learn to print later, in kindergarten, is poor practice. If he asks a direct question, the child care assistant should show him or help him to find the answer. A motivated child learns quickly. This is not to say the teacher should overdo it. The best rule of thumb is to notice the child's lead, and offer what she feels the child can handle successfully without killing his interest or enthusiasm.

COORDINATION

Control of the body follows a timetable of its own. Control of a particular muscle depends on many factors — diet, exercise, inherited ability and motivation, to name a few. A baby can control his neck and arms long before his legs. A child matures in a head-to-toe fashion. Muscles closer to the center of the body can be controlled long before those at the edges, such as hand and finger muscles. Large muscle control comes before small muscle control. Think of a toddler walking; his legs seem to swing from his hips; he is using his large hip muscle. Just as each of us starts walking and learns muscle control at different ages, each of us develops the ability to make symbols with a writing tool at different ages.

Fig. 14-3 The human figure drawn by a three year old.

Fig. 14-2 A child starts with scribbles and, when older, draws symbols of the world around him.

COGNITIVE DEVELOPMENT

Realization that there are written symbols is the first step in writing. Mental growth, which allows a child to see similarities and differences in symbols, precedes the ability to write. The child recognizes that a written mark is a shape made by a placement of lines.

A young child scribbles if given paper and a marking tool. As he grows, the scribbles are controlled into lines which the child places where he wishes, figure 14-2. With age, circles appear, then a face, later a full figure, and so on, figure 14-3. The child draws his own symbols of what he sees around him. The length of time it takes this process to develop differs with each child. Some children tie shoes, fold airplanes and use forks and spoons during preschool years. Others will not be able to do these skills until much later. This is also true with the ability to print.

In addition to muscle control, the desire to do what one sees others do, and the easy availability of writing tools are important in developing the child's ability to print. Parents can help develop a child's interest in letters by naming alphabet letters with him.

Fig. 14-4 Young children explore using writing tools.

FIRST LEARNINGS

A child may notice marks (letters) in picture books, or television may push them into view. The child observes parents or other children reading and writing. Questions and imitation follow, figure 14-4.

Letters and numbers are everywhere. "What's. that?" the child asks. Many preschoolers add alphabet letters to their drawings. Sometimes they know the name or sound of the letter.

The following early childhood activities may help the child use and gain control of small arm and finger muscles.

puzzles	painting
pegboards	chalk
beads to string	fingerpainting
small blocks	crayons, pencils and
construction toys	marking tools
cutting with scissors	

Most schools plan activities in which the child puts together or arranges small pieces. These are sometimes called table-top activities, and are available for play throughout the day. An assistant can encourage the use of table-top activities by suggestion or by having the pieces arranged invitingly on tables or shelves, figure 14-5.

Early childhood centers should create rooms that are full of symbols, letters and numbers in clear view of the child. Many toys have circles, squares, triangles and other com-

Fig. 14-5 Puzzles call for finger muscle use and control.

Fig. 14-6 Playing with toys that have alphabet letters, numerals, and symbols.

mon shapes, figure 14-6. Child care assistants can show printing in playrooms the following ways:

Labeling

Artwork
Name tags
Lockers and storage areas
Belongings
Common objects in the room such as
 scissors, paper, crayons, fishbowl,
 chair, water, etc.
School areas such as blocks, library or
 reading center, playhouse, art center,
 science center
Place cards for snacks

Display Areas

Magazine pictures with captions
Current interest displays, e.g. "Rocks
 we found on our walk"
Bulletin boards and wall displays with
 words
Alphabet guides Aa Bb
Alphabet charts
Child's work with word explanations,
 such as "Josh's block tower," or
 "Penny's clay pancakes"
Signmaking for child activities, such as
 store, hospital, wet paint, and tickets
 for sale here

Teacher-made Activities

Alphabet letters from felt, cardboard,
 sandpaper, etc.
Games with letters, numbers or symbols
Alphabet cards
Games with names and words
Greeting cards
Hats with words

The child's own name is often the first word the child prints. Parents may have taught their child to print with all capitals. Early

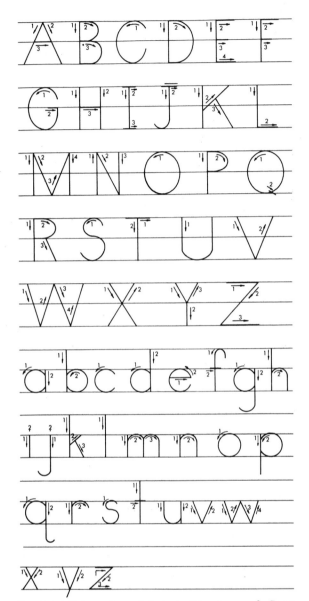

Fig. 14-7 Printscript alphabet (Courtesy of Santa Clara Unified School District, Santa Clara, California.)

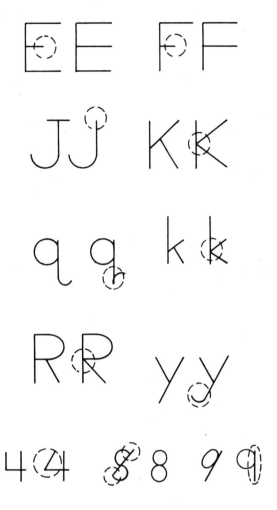

Fig. 14-8 Some geographical differences in printscript alphabet letters and numeral forms.

childhood centers then help introduce the child to the letter forms he will use in the first grades of public school.

FIRST SCHOOL ALPHABETS

In kindergarten or first grade, printing is done in printscript, sometimes called manuscript printing, figure 14-7. Centers can get samples from an elementary school in their neighborhood.

Child care assistants need to be familiar with printscript. It is easier for a child to learn the right way than to be retrained later. All printing seen by young children in a preschool should be printscript using both uppercase (capitals) and lowercase (small letters). Names, bulletin boards, and labels made by teachers should always show the correct printscript forms. Printscript letters are formed with straight lines, circles, and parts of circles. In the illustrations, the small arrows and numbers show the direction to follow in making the letters. Alphabet letters vary slightly in appearance in different parts of the country, figure 14-8.

Fig. 14-9 Printscript numerals. (Courtesy of the Santa Clara Unified School District, Santa Clara, California.)

Numbers in printed form are called numerals. Children may have used toys with numerals, such as block sets. Numbers are everywhere. The young child will probably hold up fingers to indicate his age or tell you he can count. He may start making number symbols (numerals) before showing an interest in alphabet letters. Numeral forms are available from elementary schools. The numeral forms may also be slightly different from those of another town, city, or state, figure 14-9.

EARLY ATTEMPTS

The work of young children may include letters that are sideways, backwards, or upside down. The letters may also be upright from the start. All are normal. Words may appear instead of single letters. The child may, or may not, be able to name his symbol, letter or word, figure 14-10.

Fig. 14-10 The young child may begin to put alphabet letters in his artwork.

Teachers encourage and show correct forms, but should not insist the child copy them. The teacher provides opportunities and observes the child's efforts. Making sure each child feels good about himself, whether he prints symbols or not, is an important part of teaching young children.

SUMMARY

Alphabets and printed words are part of preschool life. Centers should not try to teach all children to print. Some children may show interest, and activities are planned around this interest.

Numerals are also interesting to young children. These symbols are part of living; they are seen at school, home, and in the neighborhood. Guides for forming numerals and letters of the alphabet may be obtained from local schools. These guides may vary from city to city.

The ability to print depends upon muscle control, seeing symbols, and noting the placement of lines of the symbols.

Printscript is used in preschool, kindergarten and first grade. Letters are formed with lines and circles in upper and lowercase symbols.

Children are ready for printing at different ages. The child's knowledge of alphabet letters is individual.

Teachers sometimes help children to print. Printscript is used at early childhood centers whenever it is to be seen by children.

SUGGESTED ACTIVITIES

- Obtain a printscript guide from your local school district; inquire about cursive writing (longhand). Ask at what grade level both are used.

- Observe a preschool program, noticing and listing all written forms found in the playroom within the view of the children.

- Find some examples of young children's attempts to make symbols in their drawings. What do you notice about the symbols? Are they large, small, straight lines or slanted, capitals or small letters? Anything else noted?

- Ask three parents to print their child's name for you on a piece of paper.

- Invite a first-grade teacher to speak to the class about methods used to teach printscript in her classroom.

REVIEW

A.   Select all of the correct answers.

   1. Child care programs

       a. try to teach all children to printscript.

       b. try to teach correct printscript form.

       c. can obtain correct printscript form locally.

       d. help children with printing attempts.

   2. Small muscle control

       a. comes after large muscle control.

       b. depends on many factors.

       c. is difficult for some preschoolers.

       d. is the only thing involved in learning to print.

   3. Parents may teach a child to write his name

       a. in all capitals.

       b. because he asks them.

       c. because television has stimulated the child's interest.

       d. using both upper and lowercase letters.

   4. If drawings have upside down alphabet letters, assistant teachers should

       a. immediately begin printing lessons.

       b. suspect the child may be interested in activities with printed forms.

       c. tell the child the letters are upside down quickly.

       d. worry about the child's ability to do them perfectly.

5. A child's readiness to print may depend upon

    a. his ability to gather information from his senses.

    b. his knowing letters are formed by placing lines.

    c. his home and family.

    d. his liking the teacher.

B. Place the following in the best order. What happens first, next, last?

    1. a. small muscle control

        b. large muscle control

        c. control of fingers

    2. a. child makes letters

        b. child makes scribbles

        c. child makes circles

    3. a. teacher shows child how to make a *Y*.

        b. child knows the name of the letter *Y*.

        c. child says "Teacher make a *Y* on my paper."

    4. a. child tries to write.

        b. child sees parent writing.

        c. child prints a *b*.

    5. a. child prints letters in artwork.

        b. teacher notices and encourages.

        c. child knows the names of all the letters in the alphabet.

C. 1. What are some possible reasons why children age 2-5 years may start to print?

    2. Give examples of preschool equipment that promotes small muscle and finger control.

D. Answer the following questions.

    1. What should child care assistants consider about the printscript they use?

    2. Why is it that all preschoolers will not be interested in letters?

    3. Muscle control is only part of learning to write. Name the other factors that affect readiness for written communication.

    4. When a child says, "Is this *M*?" how should one reply?

    5. If a child is not interested in printing, what should be done?

    6. If a child says a *b* is an *f* what might a teacher say?

unit 15 practicing printscript

OBJECTIVES

After studying this unit, the student should be able to

- Make the full printscript upper and lowercase alphabet.
- List three ways printscript could be used daily.
- Describe equipment and settings which could be used for printscript development.

Equipment which can motivate interest in writing readiness should be available to children.

Scratch paper (one side already used) and crayons placed side-by-side invite use. Most local businesses or offices throw away enough scratch paper to supply preschool centers. This paper can be available every day for play activities.

Felt pens are enjoyed as a change of pace. Colored or white chalk has an appeal of its own and can be used on paper, blackboards, or cement. For variety, oil pastels which have bright colors or charcoal drawings may be used.

Most schools install child-high blackboards, figure 15-1. Table blackboards may also be available. Blackboard paint which can be easily applied to scrap wood pieces, easels, or walls is available at most local hardware stores.

Preprinting experimenting should take place in a quiet setting where the child can obtain materials from nearby shelves or storage areas. Often adjacent areas have printscript words or letters.

Letters, words, and pictures are planned for viewing on bulletin boards at children's eye level, figure 15-2. Often schools apply labels to familiar objects by making printscript signs and attaching the sign to the object with masking tape. The names of the children may appear in locker or storage areas and on personal belongings. The equipment and printed

Fig. 15-1 Child-high blackboards invite use.

Fig. 15-2 Letters and words are planned for children's viewing.

Fig. 15-3 Children's names belong in the upper left hand corner.

Fig. 15-4 Print the child's name on his work by standing behind him.

Maryellen Donald

Fig. 15-5 Letters should be large enough for the child to see easily.

words within view of the children are to offer opportunity and exposure rather than to teach.

DAILY INTERACTION

Putting the child's name on his work is the most common daily use of printscript. All names should be written in the upper left-hand corner of the paper if possible, figure 15-3. This is done to train the child to look at this spot as a preparation for reading; books are read from the left to the right margin. A child's comments about his artwork can be jotted down along the bottom or on the back of his paper. Assistants should be prepared to do this by having a dark crayon or felt tip pen in a handy place or pocket.

The child should learn and practice printing with the teacher standing behind him and working over his shoulder, figure 15-4. In this way the child sees the letters being formed in the correct position. When the child watches a teacher from a position where they are facing each other, he sees the letter going on upside down. Many teachers, time permitting, say the letters aloud as they print the child's name.

Letters or names written for the child should be about one inch or one and a half inches high for upper case, and half as long in length for lowercase. This may seem large to an adult, but the letters are much easier seen and noticed by the child when they are this size, figure 15-5.

Children may show their printing attempts, or point out the names of letters they know, to the teacher. A positive statement to the child is appropriate. "Yes, that is an *a*" or "I can see *a's, t's* and *p's*" (as she points to each). "Marie, you did print some letters."

With these comments, the teacher encourages and recognizes the child's effort. Often the child may have the wrong name or form for a letter. The child care assistant can react by saying, "It is an alphabet letter, let's go look at our alphabet and see which one."

Asking if the child would like to see the teacher make the letter is another way to supply the child with the correct form. The children will make mistakes in both making forms and naming letters and numerals. The child has many years ahead to learn. The most important thing now is that he is interested and can be supplied with correct models and encouragement.

One suggestion is to have children trace over good letter models or symbols. This can be done with crayons, felt pens, or other writing tools. Since *trace* is a word that needs explanation, the assistant will need to show the children what to do.

The teacher should ask the child if he wants his name printed on his paper. Young children can become rightly possessive over their creations, and may not want their name on the front of their papers or on them at all.

PRACTICING THE MODEL

Printscript should come automatically to the child care assistant. Practice is in order if one cannot easily and quickly print the entire alphabet in both upper and lowercase.

Without going back to the last unit, print the printscript alphabet in both upper and lowercase. Now check yourself. Be critical. Is your letter exactly like the one on page 101? If not, circle your mistake in a different color pen or pencil. Remember your local alphabet letters may vary somewhat from those in other parts of the country. Before practicing any further, obtain a local printscript guide from a neighboring elementary school if you do not already have one. The following are some correction errors made by teachers.

1. Lines should be straight — perpendicular to the edge of the paper.

2. The circular parts of small letters are half the length of large ones.

3. Circles on letters are full ones.

4. Circles and lines bisect each other.

5. Difficult ones.

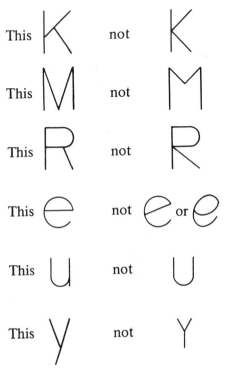

To promote interest in printscript or symbols, a child care assistant could:

- make labels for familiar objects
- make signs that fit in with child's play
  John and Jerry's Service Station
  Quiet Please
  Don't Walk on the Grass
  Cookies for Sale
- create wall displays with words
- make alphabet charts
- make charts with words
- make alphabet and number games
- make word games
- print experience stories with child dictation
- point out words in the environment
- point out symbols in the environment
- print children's names on artwork
- supply scrap paper and a variety of writing tools
- make table blackboards
- cut letters in felt, cloth, sandpaper and tagboard
- make clever nametags
- make giant alphabet letters, figure 15-6

Fig. 15-6 A teacher-made activity to promote interest in a letter of the alphabet.

PARENT COMMUNICATION

A conversation or note to the parents of a child who has asked about or started printing might include the following comments.

- Teacher has noticed the child's interest in printing alphabet letters, and/or numerals and/or words.
- Teacher is including a printscript and numeral guide for parents who wish to show their child the letter forms that he will be using in kindergarten.
- The early childhood center encourages printing attempts but does not try to teach printscript to every child. Many children are not interested and others would find it too difficult. Young children will have plenty of time and opportunity to learn printing during later years in school.
- A parent can help by having paper and writing tools for the child at home, and by noticing and praising the child when he comes to the parent with written letters.
- Children who start printing early often write letters and numerals backwards or sideways — this is to be expected.

SUMMARY

Equipment and settings for giving each child an opportunity to explore printing is available in a childhood center. Materials can be within reach. Equipment and visual printing may motivate interest.

Printscript is used in a variety of ways. The most common is in planned activities and labeling artwork. A name or sentence should start in the upper left-hand corner and move toward the right.

Assistant teachers need to examine printscript closely and practice so that good models can be supplied quickly. They are aware that encouragement and recognizing effort is more important than asking children to make correct forms.

SUGGESTED ACTIVITIES

- Obtain an order catalog from a preschool supply store or company. Most companies will send you the catalogs free of charge. Professional magazines such as *Instructor, Early Years,* and *Scholastic Teacher* are good sources for addresses. Make a list of any piece of equipment or supply item that could be used to promote printing.

- Watch children with crayons or other writing tools. Take notes. Make observations.

  a. Time spent with marking tools.

  b. Manner used — How do they hold the crayons?

  c. Would you say they had good control of both paper and tool?

- Place a pile of paper and two or three soft drawing pencils on a table. (Pencils are not used often because they need sharpening and are not always safe.) *Supervise your activity closely* — let only two or three children at a time work. How many of the children tried to make letters? How many said yes when you asked them if they wanted you to add their names to their papers?

REVIEW

A. 1. If a child comes to a child care assistant to show letters the child has drawn, how should the assistant react?

    2. If two children are arguing over the name of a letter how should the teacher handle the situation?

    3. List three ways an assistant teacher might use printscript during the day.

B. Print your local printscript alphabet in both upper and lowercase. Also print numerals 1-10.

C. In the following picture, list below all of the things the child care assistant might have done to better promote printing readiness.

D. Select the correct answers.

1. When a child's name is to be printed on his work, it should be
   a. in the center on top.
   b. in the upper right-hand corner.
   c. in the upper left-hand corner.
   d. done with an uppercase letter and lowercase letters.

2. The size of the printscript used with young children
   a. doesn't really matter.
   b. should be large enough to see.
   c. can be of any size.
   d. should be about an inch high.

3. If a teacher does not know how to form printscript letters she can
   a. practice.
   b. use her own style.
   c. get a copy from an elementary school.
   d. write instead.

E. Print your full name and address in printscript.

F. A note to the parents of a child who is interested in learning to print should include what kind of information? Give four points to bring out.

unit 16 activities with printscript

OBJECTIVES

After studying this unit, the student should be able to

- Describe a variety of printscript and symbol activities.
- Plan and present a printscript activity.

Activities in this unit deal with symbols, letters, and words. The objectives range from printscript readiness activities with symbols such as circles, squares, triangles and other geometric and common shapes, to those in which the child comes in contact with printscript letters and words.

CLAY ON PATTERNS

Purpose: Small manipulative muscle use, tracing symbols.

Materials: Clay and contact-covered cardboard sheets with patterns.

Activity: Child rolls clay and forms clay over the cardboard patterns, figure 16-1.

Fig. 16-1 Clay-on-patterns activity.

DOTS-TO-DOTS

These can be made quickly by the teacher and used as a free-play choice, figure 16-2.

Purpose: Small muscle use, forming symbols and symbol recognition.

Materials: Paper, writing tool (dittoes can be used)

Variation: Chalk and chalkboard dot patterns.

Activity: Dots are connected to form symbols.

  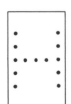 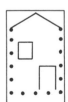

Fig. 16-2 Dots-to-Dots activity.

SORTING SYMBOLS

Purpose: Small muscle use, discriminating symbol differences, figure 16-3.

Materials: Paper, writing tool, scissors, paste.

Activity: After cutting symbols in squares from sheets, child is asked to mix them all together and then find the ones that are the same to paste on another sheet of paper.

a	a	a	o	or	△	△	△	▢
o	o	i	i		▢	▢	··	··
e	e	e	u		··	X	X	X

Variation: Teacher can make a cardboard set as a table game.

Fig. 16-3 Sorting symbols activity.

ALPHABET SONG GAME

Purpose: Recognizing letter names.

Materials: A long, printscript alphabet line.

Aa	Bb	Cc	Dd	Ee	Ff	Gg	Hh	Ii	Jj

Song: "A B C D E F G
H I J K L M N O P
Q R S T U and V
W X and Y and Z.
Now I've said my abc's,
Tell me what you think
of me."

Activity: Children sing the song while one child or the teacher touches the corresponding letter on alphabet line. Teacher can ask the group to sing slowly, quickly, in a little and big voice, in a high and then low voice.

ALPHABET POTATO PRINTS

Purpose: Recognizing letter names.

Materials: Potatoes, sharp knife (for teacher), thick paint, paper, flat containers. Teacher cuts potato halves into letters or symbols.

Activity: Prints are made by children.

ALPHABET MACARONI

Purpose: Discriminating shapes; small muscle activity.

Materials: Alphabet soup macaroni (sand, rice, salt can also be used), glue and brushes, paper, felt pen.

Activity: Child traces name by painting over lines with thinned white glue. Macaroni is then spooned over. When dry shake those that didn't stick into a container. The end

result will be raised textured letters. The teacher should demonstrate this process.

CHALK TALK

Purpose: Motivating interest in letter forms.

Materials: Chalk, chalkboard, chalkboard eraser.

Activities: Teacher presents the rhyme and drawings on the chalkboard.

Teacher's Comments

1. / One line down

2. ∧ Another this way

3. A One across
And I've drawn an A.

1. | One line down

2. P Another you see

3. B If I make another
I've made a B.

1. ○ C is very easy to make
It looks like the top of a circle cake.

2. ◒ Cut a piece for you

3. ◒ And another for me

4. C Erase them both and it's a C.

1. ○ Here's a circle

2. ⬭ I'll cut in half you see
Erase one side

3. D And there's my D.

1. □ Here's a box

2. ⊞ With 2 lines inside
Erase this part

3. E And E won't hide.

1. E This time let's start with the capital E

2. F Take away one line
And It's F you see.

1. G Gee I'm sorry
There's nothing else to do
But draw a great big G for you.

1. | | 2 lines I've drawn
Going the same way

2. ⊢ Put a line across
And it's an H I'd say.

It's time to stop here
But I'm not through
Raise your hand
Name a letter and I'll make it for you.

When the activity ends, ask if anyone would like a turn at the blackboard.

DRAWING

A line fence between children helps each to know his drawing area.

DRAW A FROG[1]

Draw two round circles (1)
And you will see
Places where
Two eyes will be.

Now make a curve (2)
And another one (3)
And a round, fat body (4)
Oh, what fun!

Draw two legs (5)
And that will do
Here's a funny
Frog for you!

[1]Virginia Sydnor Pavelko, from <u>Learning Time with Language Experience for Young Children</u>, by Louise Binder Scott, (St. Louis: McGraw-Hill Book Co.)

DRAW A FISH

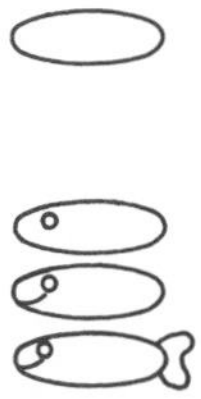

1. *I'll draw an oval*
   Like an egg in the sky
   What comes next
2. *Why it's a little eye.*
3. *Next comes a mouth*
4. *And a tail to swish*
   Look at that
   I've made a fish!

EXPERIENCE CHARTS

Purpose: Recognition that spoken words can be put in written form.

Materials: Large paper sheets (newsprint), felt pen or black crayon.

Activity: After any interesting activity such as a field trip, special speaker, party, celebration, or cooking experience, the child care assistant can suggest that a story be written about the experience. A large sheet of paper or chart sheet is hung within child's view and children dictate what happened. Teacher prints on the sheet, helping children sort out what happened first, next and last, figure 16-4.

The Picnic

We had lunch
in the park
We sat
on the grass

Fig. 16-4 An example of an experience chart.

Variation: Children sometimes like to dictate comments about paintings or other artwork. The teacher can print these on a separate sheet which will be taped to the bottom of the artwork.

OTHER CHART IDEAS

Printscript can be added to playrooms by posting charts which have been made by the teachers. Charts can be used just to look at, or can be designed to encourage the child's active involvement; pockets, parts that move, or pieces that can be added or removed, add extra interest. Charts made on heavy board or cardboard last longer. Clear contact paper may seal the surface from soil. Some ideas for charts follow.

> Color chart or number chart
> Large clock with movable hands
> Chart depicting the four seasons
> Picture story sequence charts
> Calendar
> Room task chart, "Helpers Charts"
> Texture chart (for children to feel)
> Poetry chart
> Recipe chart using step-by-step
>   illustrations
> Classification, or matching-concepts
>   chart
> Birthday charts
> Height and weight chart
> Alphabet chart

In making a chart, first draw sketches of the way words and pictures could be arranged. With a yardstick, lightly draw on guidelines with pencil. Next lightly make words in printscript. Go over printscript later with a felt pen or dark crayon. Magazines, old elementary school workbooks, old children's books, and photographs are good sources for pictures. Brads or paper fasteners make movable parts. Book pockets or heavy envelopes provide a place for cards. Commercial picture hangers with adhesive backs can be used for attaching pieces, figure 16-5.

MAGAZINE PICTURE BOOK

Purpose: Attaching word labels to pictures.

Materials: Old magazine pages, scissors, paste, construction paper, hole punch.

Activity: Child selects a picture, cuts out an object or scene, pastes it on the construction paper. Teacher asks child what words or word caption the child would like, and adds it in printscript. When dry, the labelled pictures are hole-punched and made into a book.

WORDS ON DRAWINGS

Purpose: Attaching word labels to pictures.

Materials: Felt pen or crayons.

Activity: Teacher asks each child individually if words can be added to his painting, drawing or illustration; she makes sure the child realizes the teacher is going to write on his work. It is a good idea to show the child what has been done to another child's picture beforehand. Most children will want words added, but some will not. It is best to limit this activity to the children who are making symbols of faces, figures, houses, etc. in their work. Younger children might not be able to decide if asked, "Would you like me to put a word name on something you've drawn in your picture?"

PRIMARY TYPEWRITERS

Some centers are fortunate to have primary printscript typewriters for children to examine. Children can dictate their comments to the teacher. This activity promotes recognition of printscript letters and interest in printscript.

PATTERN GUIDES (TEMPLATES)

Purpose: Small muscle use with writing tools; discrimination and recognition of shapes.

Materials: Cardboard or art board, a razor blade or art knife (for teacher's use), scissors, clear contact paper, pencil.

Variation: Plastic coffee-can lids, sharp scissors.

Construction: Draw symbol on 5 x 6 squares, cut and cover with transparent contact paper.

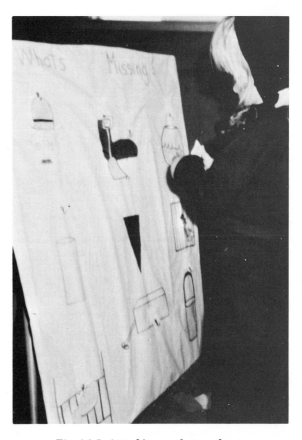

Fig. 16-5 Attaching cards to a chart.

Activity: Symbols are traced, and cut and pasted if desired.

Variation: Templates can be on blackboards. Blackboard drawings can be made with chalk and traced by the children.

TRACERS

Tracers can be used over and over again. Waxy crayons wipe off with a soft cloth, figure 16-6.

Purpose: Recognition and discrimination of symbols; small muscle coordination.

Materials: Acetate or clear vinyl sheets, cardboard, scissors, strapping or masking tape, paper, felt pen.

Construction: Attach acetate to cardboard leaving one side open to form a pocket. Make letter or word guide sheets. Simple pictures can also be used.

Fig. 16-6 Child using a tracer.

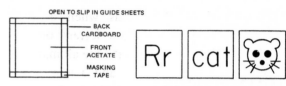

Activity: Child or teacher selects sheet and slips it into tracer pocket. A waxy crayon is used by the child to trace the guide sheet. A soft cloth erases crayon.

ALPHABET BINGO

Purpose: Recognition and discrimination of letters.

Materials: Cardboard, felt pen, scissors, pencil, ruler, paper, old pack of playing cards, glue, clear contact paper.

Construction: Cardboard is cut to make four or more 8½ x 11-inch sheets (any similar size is also suitable). Each sheet is divided into nine or twelve sections. An alphabet letter is added to each section. Make sure each sheet has a different combination of letters. Cover sheet with clear contact paper. Turning to the pack of old playing cards, glue paper to the front side of each playing card. Add letters of the alphabet. Covering with clear contact will make these cards more durable. For markers, cut paper into small pieces; bottle caps or poker chips may also be used.

Activity: Teacher passes out the sheets to the children. She holds up a playing card (with a letter on it) and asks if any child has that letter on his sheet. If so, the child should cover it with a marker.

A game ends when a child covers all the letters on his sheet. At that time all markers are removed and a new game begins. The child who wins the game by being the first to cover all his letters takes the place of the teacher and holds up the playing cards for the next game.

Fig. 16-7 "His and Hers" activity.

FANFOLDS

These can be set up on tables or in reading centers. They can create an interest in letters and words whether the child interacts, or only looks. It is really a series of small chart ideas.

Purpose: Recognition of symbols, words and names.

Materials: A wide variety of materials can be used, pictures, yardage scraps, mirrors, nature items, yarn, string, shoelaces, book pockets, cards, etc. Felt pens, ruler, scissors, glue, strapping tape.

Construction: Make a line of cardboard sheets. Join with strapping tape at edges leaving a half-inch gap between each sheet so sheet can fold flat for storage.

Fanfolds stand by themselves in accordion style.

Ideas for the front or back of sheets.

HIS AND HERS

Purpose: To help children learn to form letters and write legibly, figure 16-7.

Materials: Cardboard, paper clips, writing paper, scissors, clear contact paper.

Construction: Cut a 13 x 15-inch piece of cardboard. Place a 9 x 12-inch sheet of writing paper on the cardboard close to the bottom. Just above the top of the paper in the center of the board, cut out a rectangular shape. Put a paper clip through this opening and slip the writing paper under the clip. Print (or write) the child's name on a strip of the writing paper, place it above the opening in the cardboard, and cover it with clear contact paper.

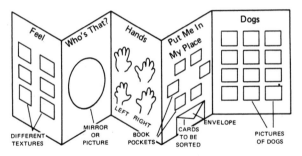

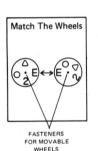

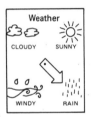

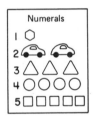

Activity: The child may now use this pad to practice writing his name. Make similar practice pads for words, sentences, or paragraphs. (Note: Using clear contact on handmade learning devices will make them last longer. It is great for preserving magazine pictures, too.)[1]

[1]Reprinted with permission of the publishers, Allen Raymond, Inc. Darien, Conn. 06820, EARLY YEARS Magazine, January, 1973.

SUGGESTED ACTIVITIES

- Collect five printscript activity ideas from other resource books or create them yourself. Use the following format.

Title   Activity

Purpose   Construction (if any)

Materials   Variations (if any)

- Make up three original charts.

- Make a preschool chart, include some printscript words. Bring it to the next class meeting.

- Use one of the activities from this unit with a group of children, or with one child, and answer the following questions.

    Was it of interest to the child or children?
    What was the purpose of the activity?
    How were printscript letters or symbols used?
    Were the children successful in the activity?

- Originate your own chalk talk. A rhyme or simple story works well. Try out your creation on young children, and write a description of the children's reactions.

- Make up an experience chart after taking a small group of children on a walk.

REVIEW

A. 1. Name common symbols that might be used in designing activities with symbols.

2. By whom are experience charts or stories dictated and written?

3. Make a list of materials and tools useful in chart making.

4. What is the purpose of a line fence between children during blackboard activities.

Section 5 Reading

unit 17 readiness for reading

OBJECTIVES

After studying this unit, the student should be able to

- Describe reading readiness.
- List three methods used to teach reading.
- Discuss the child care assistant's role in reading.

No two children learn exactly the same way or at the same age. At one time it was thought there was an age when all children became ready for reading instruction. Ideas have changed. Now one can find children who read in early childhood centers and kindergartens. Some have picked up the skill on their own; others have spent time with an older brother or sister, parents, teachers, or other family members. Reading is considered the fourth language art.

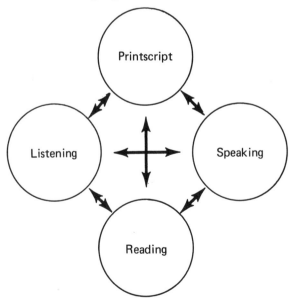

Fig. 17-1 The four language arts are interrelated and interdependent.

READING

A language arts approach to reading views reading as one part of the communication process. The language arts are interrelated, not separate, isolated skills. The child care assistant teacher should make every effort to show the relationship between the various areas of language arts by giving the child the complete picture. In other words, the goal in a language arts approach to language development is to promote the child's understanding that communication is a total picture in which speaking, listening and written symbols and the reading of those symbols are logically connected, figure 17-1.

At one time the connection between listening, speaking, written words and reading was overlooked. The subjects were often taught in schools as separate skills, and the natural connection between each area was not clear to children. In a language arts approach, the connection (the way these areas fit together) is emphasized.

The Task Force Report on Early Childhood Education by the State of California (1971) states:

Concern should be given to the nature of the written language material used in early reading instruction and the degree of fit between this material and the child's

119

oral language style. Attention should also be devoted to representing the child's oral language in written form with very little teacher editing. In this way the child comes to understand the relationship between speech and writing as a basis for reading instruction.

The child care assistant realizes certain skills and abilities appear in children before other skills and abilities appear. These early learnings in listening and speaking serve as beginnings for further language and communication, figure 17-2.

Fig. 17-2   Early experience in language arts can serve as a basis for developing reading skills.

Fig. 17-3   An interest in books can lead to an interest in printed words.

Activities with young children can move easily from listening, speaking, seeing or using printscript, to beginning attempts at reading.

It is not uncommon to have preschool youngsters who can read most of the names of the children in their group after being exposed to an activity in which the children's names are used.

Although early childhood centers rarely offer formal reading instruction, some young children can read. The ability to read is present if the child understands and acts appropriately when he sees a printed word.

Most teachers have had children read to them from a favorite, memorized storybook. However, a word from the book could not be recognized out of context and really read by the child when he sees it elsewhere.

A child may develop the ability to recognize words through an interest in printing letters. Another child may pick up the sounds of alphabet letters through listening and finding words that start with the same letter. Often these letters sound and look alike. Interest in books and stories can lead children into early interest and recognition of words, figure 17-3. Some children have the ability to distinguish one word from another word by sight and can easily remember words.

Early readers tend to have a desire to read. They also have had the opportunities and interactions with others who have answered their questions and stimulated their interest. A few children will read between the ages of four and five, but many will not have the capability or interest to read until a later age. There is no doubt that learning to read involves a variety of skills which are interwoven in the other three areas of language arts. The child who has reading readiness can be defined as one who has displayed some success in reading a few words.

READINESS SKILLS

A teacher should be aware of each child's interest and capacity. In daily observations and verbal conversations during planned and unplanned times, a child's responses give valuable clues, figure 17-4. The wrong answers are as important as the right ones.

Some language activities include the introduction and practice of skills that will be used when the child learns to read. These are often called *reading readiness activities.* Readiness may be defined as a state that allows one to proceed without hesitation, delay or difficulty. Readiness includes skills, motivation, desire and attitudes concerning the task, and how the child feels about himself. Reading is a complex task which involves eye and hand muscles. It requires a degree of reasoning ability (mental maturity) and a degree of motor (physical) development.

The ideal situation for a child learning to read would be a one-to-one child/teacher ratio with the reading task suited to the child's individual capacity, learning style and individual interests. This is difficult to fulfill in an early childhood learning center due to the number of children per teacher and the many other duties required of a teacher. Another factor is the teacher's limited training and knowledge of a variety of methods to teach reading.

OBJECTIVES

A list of objectives for reading readiness follows:

- Acquiring the ability to listen
- Building vocabulary through first-hand experiences

  . . recognizing likenesses and differences

  . . identifying through sight and sound

  . . rhyming

  . . increasing memory span

  . . recalling sequence and content

  . . following directions

- Increasing speech output

  . . developing attitudes of each child's ability and worth

  . . increasing imaginative and creative speech

- Building critical thinking and problem solving with language

  . . identifying through clues

  . . classifying, sorting and organizing

  . . concept and relationship development

  . . anticipating outcomes

  . . seeing cause and effect relations

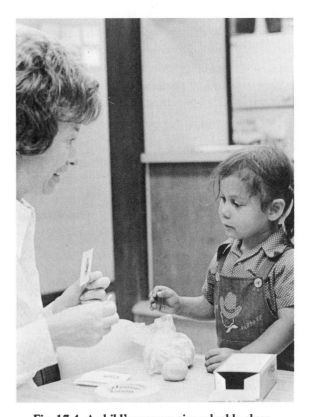

Fig. 17-4 A child's answers give valuable clues.

- Developing self-confidence

    . . attitudes of self-competence

- Increasing interest and motivation through enjoyment and success in language activities

- Developing left and right awareness

- Developing positive attitudes toward books and skills in book use

    . . turning pages

    . . storage and care

- Recognizing incongruities

    . . the ability to see the lack of fitness in a situation or statement, such as "The mouse swallowed the elephant."

- Recognizing context clues

    . . realizing that pictures on the same page give visual clues to the words.

METHODS

There are many methods in which reading skills can be taught to young children. Educators agree there is no one best way for every child. Each elementary school decides which method, or methods will be used in that particular school.

Most of the children who do read during preschool years have learned words through a "look and say" method. That is, when they see the written letters of their name or another word they can identify the name or word. They have recognized and memorized that group of symbols. It is felt that children who learn words in this fashion have memorized the *shape* of the word for they often confuse words with similar outlines such as *Jane* for *June*. They may not know the alphabet names of the letters or the sounds of each letter (phonics). In a phonetic approach to reading, the child breaks the word into sounds and decodes it.

A language arts approach to reading introduces children to written words through their own interests in play; through their enjoyment of using oral language (speaking); and

through listening to language. Often the child's first experience with written words comes from his own speech and actions. A sign that says "John's block tower" or "Free Kittens" may be a child's first exposure to reading. Emphasis is upon the fact that words are part of daily living, rather than that words are only important during planned reading instruction in school.

Dolores Durkin puts it in this way[1]

> The term 'language arts' is school talk and refers to the combination of listening, speaking, reading and writing. It thus encompasses all aspects of verbal communication. For this textbook it is a most important term because it is at the core of two of its assumptions: (a) the major academic responsiblity of those who teach in the primary grades, but also in the school years preceding first grade, lies with the language arts; and (b) one productive way to promote skill in reading among younger children is through attention to all the dimensions of verbal communication.

Speaking directly to teachers of young children she strongly recommends:

> If pre-first grade teachers are either unwilling or unable to offer opportunities to learn to read that are interesting and appropriate for young children, they should forget about reading and simply continue with their traditional programs.

PARENTS AND READING READINESS

Parents often are interested in ways to help their children succeed in school. Since the ability to read is an important factor in early schooling, parents may seek the advice of the teacher.

Many programs keep parents informed of both the school's program and goals, and their child's progress. Early childhood centers realize that parents and teachers working together can produce a carryover between things learned at home and at school.

Following are suggestions for parents who wish to help their children's language skills. Many are similar to suggestions for teachers in early childhood centers. It should be pointed

[1] Dolores Durkin, Teaching Young Children to Read (Boston: Allyn and Bacon, Inc., 1972.)

Fig. 17-5 All answers are right answers according to each child's individual observations and experiences.

out that all children's answers are right according to their individual perceptions and experience.

- Show an interest in what your child has to say. Answer, giving clear, descriptive, full statements in response.
- Arrange for your child to have playmates and to meet and talk to people of all ages.
- Make your child feel secure. Encourage and accept his opinions and feelings.
- Develop a pleasant voice and offer the best model of speech you can. Shouting and loud voices can create tension.
- Encourage your child to listen and to explore by feeling, smelling, seeing and tasting when possible.
- Enjoy new experiences. Talk about them as they happen. Every community has places of interest to visit for the young child — parks, stores, museums, zoos, buses, trains, etc., figure 17-6.
- Read to your child and tell him stories. Stop when interest wanes. Try to develop a liking for books, and a knowledge of how to care for them. Provide a quiet place for your child to enjoy books on his own.
- Listen to what your child is trying to say rather than how it is said. Correct in a

Fig. 17-6 A library can become a familiar place to visit.

relaxed manner, remembering too much correction may stop his talking.

- Have confidence in his abilities. Patience and encouragement help language skills grow. Some of his speech sounds will probably not be clear until age 7 or 8.
- Consult a specialist (speech therapist) or your child's teacher if you feel your child is more than two years behind, or different, in his development of language.

SUMMARY

The fourth area of the language arts is reading. Although early childhood centers rarely offer reading instruction, some preschoolers can read.

The goal of the child care assistant is to blend the language arts skills — listening, speaking, reading, and printscript experiences. One activity can connect and flow into another activity in a natural way, giving young children a clearer picture of communication.

Experiences in language provide a background for reading readiness. The "look and say" method, the phonetic method and the language arts approach are three methods. Working with parents can help language development at home and at school.

SUGGESTED ACTIVITIES

- Invite a kindergarten teacher and a first-grade teacher to discuss their experiences and knowledge about young children and reading.

- Observe a kindergarten. List and describe any activities which you felt would increase a child's reading readiness.

- Make a series of printscript words (common ones such as dog, cat, and highly advertised words such as Coca Cola, and Rice Krispies; include children's names found at a local preschool). Test these words on a group of four year olds in a "game-like" way. Describe the children's response to your game.

- Create an activity in which

  (a) speaking and printscript both occur.
  (b) listening and printscript both occur.
  (c) printscript and reading both occur.

- In a small group, discuss what you would do and what your limitations would be, if you were working with a group of young children and found that two of them were reading a few words.

REVIEW

A. Discuss the following situations briefly.

  1. A child asks you to listen to him read his favorite book.

  2. You have noticed a young child who is able to read all of the printscript in the playroom.

  3. A mother notices her child is reading a few words and asks advice as to what to do.

B. How can a child care assistant include the four language arts in activities?

C. Explain what is meant by:

Reading	Phonics
Readiness	Incongruities
Method	

D. Select the phrase which *best* completes the following sentences.

  1. During ages 4 and 5 years

    a. many children learn to read.
    b. a few children learn to read.
    c. children should be given reading instruction.
    d. most children will be ready to read.

2. The language arts are
   a. reading, printscript, and listening.
   b. speaking, reading, and listening.
   c. listening, speaking, printscript (writing), and reading.
   d. reading readiness, listening, speaking, and alphabet knowledge.

3. Children may begin reading
   a. because they have an interest in alphabet letters.
   b. because they have an interest in books.
   c. because they want to see what they say written down.
   d. because of an interest in speaking, listening, or writing (print-script).

4. Reading readiness
   a. includes a variety of skills, motives, and attitudes.
   b. can be defined as showing an interest in reading.
   c. means at a certain age a child will perfect all the skills he needs to read.
   d. means child care assistants should teach reading to most children.

5. Parents and early childhood teachers work together
   a. so parents will teach their children to read at home.
   b. so teachers can teach reading during preschool years.
   c. so *at home* learnings and *at school* learnings are understood by both parents and teachers.
   d. so that children will have the same experiences at home that takes place at school.

unit 18 resources for language development materials

OBJECTIVES

After studying this unit, the student should be able to

- Explain the need for materials in language development activities.
- Assist teachers in the care, storage and replacement of materials.
- Discuss the assessment of language ability and role of the assistant.

In many sections of this textbook, materials to promote language development is based on a number of reasons:

- Words are symbols for objects and ideas.
- Young children gain knowledge through their sense organs.
- The young child enjoys the physical activity of handling objects and exploring situations.
- Materials can motivate play and communication with other children and adults.
- A change of materials keeps a center an interesting and vital place where there is lots to talk about.

TYPES OF MATERIALS

Materials can be described as objects or items used by either teachers or children.

Fig. 18-1 Children playing with a teacher-made card game.

Materials may be staff made or commercially made.

STAFF-MADE MATERIALS

Every center has budget limitations. Staff-made items can increase the variety of materials available for language development activities, figure 18-1.

Many materials are creatively designed for special language-teaching purposes. Other materials have been made from ideas obtained from other centers, other teachers, commercially-manufactured items, resource magazines, or teacher workshops.

Staff-made materials are based on the interests and developmental levels found in a particular group of children. Materials can be devised and designed to motivate and stimulate. This is part of the challenge of teaching — to keep a program continually inviting, expanding, and interesting to a unique group of individual children.

Some materials are made for teacher use only. Other materials are used by both teachers and children. Still others are made solely for child use, figure 18-2.

The Child Care Assistant's Role

As a member of the staff, the child care assistant's role in providing staff-made materials includes:

- designing and creating appropriate materials.

Fig. 18-2 Some materials are designed for children to use without teacher's help.

Fig. 18-3 Teacher-made materials are welcomed by teachers and children.

- construction and preparation of materials.

- use of materials with children.

- care, storage and replacement of existing materials.

Appropriateness, expense, and sturdiness must be considered in the design and construction of materials. Most teacher-made materials are appreciated and welcomed by the entire staff, and enjoyed by the children, figure 18-3.

COMMERCIALLY DEVELOPED MATERIALS

There is a wide variety of commercially-manufactured materials for early childhood language development. Materials are available from teachers' supply stores and from a great number of educational media and equipment companies. Pictures, books, puppets, games, toys, audiovisual items, and idea resource books for early childhood teachers are just a few of the many materials manufactured.

Companies send free catalogs to interested people upon request. Teacher magazines are a good source for addresses.

In addition to single items, kits and sets are made specifically to promote language development. Kits and sets may include pictures, objects, games, charts, puppets, and audiovisual aids, such as records, filmstrips and films.

Most large kits include a teacher's manual with daily, planned suggestions and directions for a language–development program. The goals of each activity may be explained in detail along with suggested teacher behavior, and specific directions instructing what the teacher is to say during the activity. Most of the kits are based on sound educational principles and have been designed by early childhood educators. Many of the kits are sequential in nature, starting with basic language arts skills and progressing to more mature levels. Often the set has been developed for use with language disadvantaged children. Goals cited in kits and sets include:

- Vocabulary development.

- Development of thought processes and problem-solving techniques.

- Practice with basic sentence patterns of Standard English.

- Use of existing syntax and new syntax patterns.

- Interpretation of feelings and points of view.

- Use of creative language.

- Providing enjoyment and development of positive attitudes.

- Development of a self-concept.

- Teaching of Standard English as a second language.

Teachers are divided on the use of language development kits. Some prefer one kit over another; others prefer to plan all of their own program. Teachers often combine kit activities with self-planned ideas. Many have expressed concern that a kit or set should not become the total program. If this should happen, language arts might be offered only one way and at only one time of the day. They also point out that activities should be planned with awareness of a particular group's current interests, and should relate to the children's past experiences. Kits that are based on the life experiences of children who live in large cities may lack reality for rural children, just as kits based on the familiar experiences of the middle-class child would not be appropriate for children in poverty areas.

Care, proper storage, repair and replacement of commercial language development materials is usually part of the child care assistant's duties. Some kits are quite costly, making teacher use, storage and care even more important.

COMMERCIAL ASSESSMENT INSTRUMENTS

The commercial assessment instruments (tests, rating scales, and checklists) in language development are used to find a child's achievement level. With this information a teacher can plan activities that provide a greater chance of promoting growth. Early childhood centers often try to determine the center's effectiveness by rating children at both the beginning and ending of a school year. When this is done with a young child at the beginning of his first experience in a group situation (and possibly his first time away from his home setting,) results may not be favorable or accurate. Bernard Spodek points out:[1]

[1]Bernard Spodek, Teaching in the Early Years, Prentice-Hall, Inc., (Englewood Cliffs: New Jersey), 1972.

"Administration of tests early in a child's career has certain inherent pitfalls. Many young children are unfamiliar with testing procedures and do not know appropriate response behavior, thus making test results invalid. It may be well to postpone administering tests to young children until they have been in school long enough to have been acculturated to the ways of the school."

A child care assistant may have the responsibility of administering a test to a group of young children. This may be accomplished by taking each child aside and asking him to answer questions or perform tasks. The teacher or assistant must have a clear understanding of the test's instruction manual beforehand.

Many different types of tests are manufactured. Some are designed to give a picture of the child's ability in a number of language and communication areas; others may be limited to one skill.

Tests are often standardized for large groups of children. In this case, it may be possible to compare one child to a great many other children of the same age.

DAILY OBSERVATION

Teacher observation is one of the best tools in determining individual skills. However, many teachers do not have the time to do a great many observations of individual children because they have other duties. Daily happenings give important clues for the planning of growth producing activities. Planned experiences, and the opportunity to play and talk with other children and adults should lead to each child's enjoyment and skill in the language arts, figure 18-4.

SUMMARY

A variety of materials and media is used to promote language development in early childhood centers.

Materials can:

- motivate and stimulate.

- promote play and interaction.

- introduce new learnings.

- keep children interested.

- provide variety.

- offer opportunities to manipulate and explore.

Materials can be made by staff members or purchased. Staff-made items help provide a variety of activities. The needs, motivations and interests of a particualr group serve as the basis for the design of sturdy and inexpensive materials.

Commercial language-development kits and sets are available. They differ in goals, activity plans, and numbers and types of items included. Most are sequential in nature, starting with the simple and moving toward higher and broader levels of development. Teacher manuals should be studied closely before using the kits for an understanding of directions and suggestions.

A child care assistant sometimes administers commercial assessment materials. Knowing the abilities of the child may make it

Fig. 18-4 Observations give teachers clues for planning uses for materials.

possible to match activities to individual needs. Tests are also given to measure the effectiveness of a program. Observations of children's speech and behavior provide clues that are helpful in planning appropriate activities.

SUGGESTED ACTIVITIES

- Visit an early childhood center; list and describe staff-made materials for language development.

- In small groups, compare language-development materials found in catalogs. Make comparisons between companies. Find 5 to 10 items your group feels would be valuable for a center's language-development program.

- Visit a local stationary and supply store. Describe five items or materials one could use in developing staff-made materials, or describe five commercially manufactured language-development materials or media.

- Develop a list and description of language-development kits used in local programs.

- Obtain a language kit. Read the teacher's manual and outline the goals of the program. Present an activity in class using other students in the role of the children.

- Invite an early childhood teacher to speak to the class describing her use of teacher-made and commercially-made materials.

- Invite a manufacturer's representative of an early childhood language kit to describe his products to the class.

- Study the publisher's instructions and administer a language-development assessment instrument to three different children (ages 2 – 5 years). In what ways could the results serve as a basis for activity planning? List your answers.

- Ask an early childhood teacher to speak about the use of assessment instruments in her program.

- Ask a school psychologist to describe testing and test construction.

REVIEW

A. Briefly discuss the following statements:

1. Many different types of media and materials are used to promote language arts in young children.

2. A child care assistant can add to a center's program by being aware of commercial materials for use in the language arts.

3. In designing and constructing materials for young children, there are important considerations.

4. Part of a child care assistant's duties includes the care of materials.

B. Match items in Column I with Column II. Choose statements that are *best* suited to the items.

I	II
1. Publisher's Test Instructions	a. Free upon request
2. Tests	b. Daily happenings
3. Teacher observation	c. Usually less expensive
4. Staff-made items	d. A construction concern
5. Sturdiness	e. Storage, proper use, and replacement
6. Care	f. Assessment instruments
7. Catalogs	g. A collection of teaching materials
8. Kit or set	h. Studied before administering
9. Goals	i. From simple to complex
10. A sequence	j. Objectives of use

C. In the use of commercial language-development kits or sets, discuss what you think are positive features and what you feel might be negative features.

D. Select the one *best* answer.

1. A large quantity of language materials

   a. makes a center interesting to young children.
   b. may not make a center interesting unless materials are also appropriate.
   c. assures language arts will be enjoyed.
   d. makes variety and appropriateness possible.

2. Test results are

   a. always valid if a test is standardized.
   b. used primarily to judge children's inherited ability.
   c. used to help teachers plan growing experiences.
   d. reliable if the child care assistant has studied the publisher's instructions.

3. Materials can be purchased

   a. as single items or in groups.
   b. directly from manufacturers.
   c. at teacher's supply stores.
   d. at all of the aforementioned sources.

4. Before administering a test to a young child, the child care assistant

   a. needs to know how to score the test.
   b. must have read the testing instructions carefully.
   c. needs to know if the test was standardized.
   d. should know that most tests are really used to judge a teacher's effectiveness.

5. Language-development kits should be used

   a. without question as they are usually made by educators.
   b. as the total language program.
   c. when the staff wants a sequential program.
   d. when staff members clearly understand goals and methods.

APPENDIX

THE LITTLE ELF WHO LISTENS

Author Unknown

Do you know what an elf is? No one ever saw an elf, but we can pretend it is a little boy about the size of a squirrel. This elf I'm going to tell you about lived at the edge of a big woods.

He played with chattering chipmunks, with bushy-tailed squirrels, and with hopping rabbits. They were his best friends.

Now, this little elf had something very special. His fairy godmother had given him *three pairs* of listening ears! That would be *six* ears, wouldn't it?

There was a *big* pair of ears, a *middle-sized* pair of ears, and a *tiny* pair of ears.

When the little elf wore his *big* ears, he could hear the faintest (smallest) sounds in the woods — leaves falling from the trees, the wind whispering to the flowers, the water rippling over stones in the little stream. He could hear the dogs barking far, far away. The little elf always told his friends, the squirrels, the chipmunks, and the rabbits, about the dogs, so they could run and hide. They were very thankful.

The little elf wore his *tiny* ears when the storms came and the wind blew loud and fierce, and when the thunder roared and crashed. The little animals, who had only one pair of ears apiece, were frightened by the loud noises, but their friend, the elf, told them that the wind and the thunder were important. After them would come the rain, and the rain was needed to help the food to grow.

Most of the time the little elf wore his *middle-sized* ears. He liked them best of all. He listened to all the middle-sized sounds with them, not the very loud and not the very soft sounds.

One morning some children came to the woods to pick flowers. "What shall we do with our pretty flowers?" a little girl asked.

A boy called Billy said, "Let's take them to school." "Let's!" the little girl agreed. "We can show them to the other children."

The little elf listened, and he wished that he could go to school. He wanted to see and hear what the children did at school.

He told his friends, the squirrels, the chipmunks and the rabbits, about it, but they said, "No, an elf can't go to school. School is just for children."

The little elf decided he would go to school anyway. So the next morning he crept out of his warm bed of leaves under the toadstool and skippety-skipped down the road toward the school.

Soon he came to a big building. Girls and boys were playing out on the playground. There was a red, white and blue flag flying high on a pole, so the little elf knew this was really the school.

Just then a bell rang, and the children all went inside. The little elf quietly slipped inside too.

You were the girls and boys playing outside. You are the children that the little elf followed.

Which pair of ears do you think he will have to use?

— His *big* ears because you talk too low, as if you were afraid of your own voice?

— His *tiny* ears because you talk so loud that you sound like a thunderstorm?

— Or his *middle-sized* ears because you are talking just right — loud enough so everyone in the room can hear, but not so loud that you seem to be shouting? Remember, the little elf likes his *middle-sized* ears best!

Suggestion: It's a good idea to show tiny, middle-sized and big ears drawn on the chalkboard or on paper, or on the flannelboard.

(A followup to this story could be sorting objects into three groups by size.)

LITTLE DUCK[1]

A good group participation story. Children imitate the actions with teacher.

Run	=	Slap thighs quickly.
Walk	=	Slap thighs slowly.
Big Steps	=	Thump fists on chest.
Swim	=	Rub palms of hands together rapidly.
Bang	=	Clap hands once.

Little Duck was scolded for eating too many bugs, so he said to his mother, "I am going to run away. Then I can eat anything I like."

So Little Duck left the barnyard and his own dear mother who loved him. He walked down the road on his little flat feet. (Action)

Little Duck met a cow who was munching hay.

"Have some," offered the cow.

Hay was much too rough for Little Duck to eat because he had no teeth to chew it. He thanked the cow for her thoughtfulness and walked on. (Action) Suddenly, he heard a big BANG. (Clap) Little Duck trembled with fright.

"Oh, oh, that must be a hunter with a gun," he cried.

Little Duck ran away from there fast. (Action) Then Little Duck heard some BIG, LOUD steps coming toward him. (Action) He hid in some bushes until the big steps went by.

"Why, that was only a HORSE," said Little Duck happily.

Little Duck met a dog with a bone.

"Have some," said the dog.

"No, thank you," said Little Duck as he walked on. (Action)

Little Duck came to a pond. He jumped into the water and swam across the pond. (Action) He climbed out of the water and walked on. (Action)

Suddenly Little Duck heard a fierce sound, "Grrrrrowl, Rrrrrruff."

Right in front of Little Duck sat a fox!

"Yum, yum," said the fox, smacking his lips. "Duck for dinner!"

"Oh, oh!" cried Little Duck as he began to run. (Action)

He ran and ran faster and faster. (Action) He came to the pond and swam across. (Action) The fox was right behind him.

Suddenly there was a loud BANG. (Action) When the fox heard the big noise, he turned and ran away. (Action)

Little Duck felt safer now, but he kept right on running. (Action)

---

[1] Louise Binder Scott from <u>Learning Time with Language Experiences for Young Children</u>, (New York: McGraw-Hill, 1968)

He passed the horse — and the cow — and the dog with a bone. Soon he was back in the barnyard with his own dear mother who loved him.

He said:

"I'm a little duck as you can see,
And this barnyard is the best place for me."

Little Duck knew that being scolded was for his own good, and he never ate too many bugs again. He never ran away again, either.

Ask: "What made the big bang?"

I'M GOING TO CATCH A LION FOR THE ZOO

I'll get up in the morning (yawn and stretch)

I'll put on my clothes (go through motions)

I'll take a long piece of rope down from the wall (reach up)

I'll carry it over my shoulder (push up arm to shoulder)

Open the door (pretend to turn door handle)

And close the door (clasp hands)

I'm going on a lion hunt, and I'm not afraid (slap hands on knees)

Whoops — comin' to a hill (climbing with hands)

Now I'm crossing a bridge (pound closed fists on chest)

And I'm crossing a river (motion as though swimming)

Now I'm going thru tall grass (rub hands together)

Whoops — I'm walking in mud (poke air-filled cheeks)

I'm going on a lion hunt, and I'm not afraid (slap hands on knees)

Comin' to a lion territory — want to catch a lion

With green stripes and pink polka dots

Have to go tippy-toe (finger tips on knees)

I'm climbing up a tree (climb up and look all around)

No lion!

Going in a dark cave (cup hands around eyes and look around)

Oh, a lion!

(The trip back home is exactly the same, only in reverse and faster. *The cave* is first and *slam the door* is last)

Home at last. I'm not going on any more lion hunts. I've found a lion, and I'm afraid.

(This story is full of child participation and action. It takes teacher practice, but is well worth the effort.)

HOW SAMMY SNAKE GETS A NEW SKIN[2]
by Pauline C. Peck

"My skin is too small,"
  said Sammy Snake.
"I need a new skin."
  Sammy met Toby Turtle.
"I need a new skin,"
  said Sammy.
"Where can I get one?"
"I don't know," said Toby,
"I never need a new skin."
  Sammy met Katy Caterpillar.
"I need a new skin,"
  said Sammy.
"Where can I get one?"
"I know," said Katy.
"Spin a cocoon, the way I do."
"I can't do that," said Sammy.
  And he slid away.
  Sammy met Grampa Snake.
"I need a new skin,"
  said Sammy.
"Where can I get one?"
"I know," said Grampa.
"You just wiggle and wiggle."
Sammy wiggled and wiggled.
He wiggled his old skin right off!
And do you know what?
Underneath his old skin
there was a shiny new skin
that was JUST RIGHT!

---

[2] Special permission granted by <u>My Weekly Reader I,</u> published by Xerox Education Publications, Xerox Corporation, 1968.

THE LION AND THE MOUSE

Pieces:	Lion Awake	Tree	Mouse
	Lion Sleeping	Rope	Two Hunters
Action:	See story in Unit 9.		

Patterns from <u>Adventures in Felt</u> by Jeanne M. Machado (C. 1972)

The Lion and the Mouse (Continued)

THE SEED

Pieces:	Small Roots	Seed	Beaver
	Green Shoot	Bird	Large Tree
	Deer	Small Trunk	Apples (5 or 6)
	Mr. Man	Leaves	

Action: See story in Unit 9.

Cut as one piece

APPLE AND WORM

Pieces: Apple, Worm

Action: Move the worm to fit the following positional words:

in	on	front	side	bottom	behind
out	off	back	top	under	etc.

THE HARE AND THE TORTOISE
Adapted from Aesop

Pieces: Rabbit   Dog   Rabbit running   Finish Line   Tree
          Turtle   Hen   Rabbit sleeping   Flag

The Hare and the Tortoise
(Continued)

One day the rabbit was talking to some of the other animals; "I am the fastest runner in the forest," he said. "I can beat anyone! Do you want to race?"

"Not I," said the dog.

"Not I," said the hen.

"I will race with you," said the turtle.

"That's a good joke," said the rabbit. "I could dance around you all the way and still win."

"Still bragging about how fast you are," answered the turtle. "Come on, let's race. Do you see that flag over there? That will be the finish line. Hen, would you stand by the flag so that you can tell who wins the race?"

"Dog, will you say the starting words — get on your mark, get ready, get set, go!"

"Stand there," said the dog. "Get on your mark, get ready, get set, go!"

The rabbit ran very fast. He looked over his shoulder and saw how slowly the turtle was running on his short little legs. Just then he saw a shady spot under a tree. He thought to himself — that turtle is so slow I have time to rest here under this tree. So he sat down on the cool grass, and before he knew it, he was fast asleep.

While he slept, the turtle was running. (Clump, Clump — Clump, Clump) He was not running very fast, but he kept on running. (Clump, Clump — Clump, Clump) Pretty soon the turtle came to the tree where the rabbit was sleeping. He went past and kept on running. (Clump, Clump — Clump, Clump)

The turtle was almost to the finish line. The hen saw the turtle coming and said, "Turtle, keep on running. You've almost won the race."

When the hen spoke, the rabbit awoke. He looked down by the finish line and saw the turtle was almost there. As fast as he could, rabbit started running again. Just then he heard the hen say, "The turtle is the winner!"

"But I'm the fastest," said the rabbit.

"Not this time," said the hen. "Sometimes slow and steady wins the race."

Put on turtle, dog, hen, rabbit at left edge of board.

Add finishing line flag on right edge of board. Move hen by flag.

Put on running rabbit. Remove standing rabbit.

Add sleeping rabbit while removing running rabbit.

Change sleeping rabbit to running rabbit.

FIVE YELLOW DUCKLINGS
(A Flannelboard Poem)

Pieces: 5 Yellow Ducklings   1 Mother Duck   1 Pond (large enough for 5 ducklings)

Special permission granted by Adventures in Felt ©1972 by Jeanne M. Machado.

Five yellow ducklings went swimming one day,
Across the pond and far away.
Old mother duck said, "Quack, Quack, Quack,"
Four yellow ducklings came swimming back.

Place pond, mother duck and 5 ducklings on flannelboard. Remove 1 duckling.

Four yellow ducklings went swimming one day,
Across the pond and far away.
Old mother duck said, "Quack, Quack, Quack,"
Three yellow ducklings came swimming back.

Remove 1 duckling.

Three yellow ducklings went swimming one day,
Across the pond and far away.
Old mother duck said, "Quack, Quack, Quack,"
Two yellow ducklings came swimming back.

Remove 1 duckling.

Two yellow ducklings went swimming one day,
Across the pond and far away.
Old mother duck said, "Quack, Quack, Quack,"
One little duckling came swimming back.

Remove 1 duckling.

One yellow duckling went swimming one day,
Across the pond and far away.
Old mother duck said, "Quack, Quack,Quack,"
No little ducklings came swimming back.
Old mother duck said, "Quack, Quack, Quack," (very loudly)
Five yellow ducklings came swimming back.

Remove last duckling.

Add 5 ducklings.

Suggestions:

Have children listen and participate when mother duck says "Quack, Quack, Quack." The last "Quack, Quack, Quack" should be louder than the first five. This is a good poem for children to dramatize. Outline a pond area with chalk, tape, or use an old blue blanket. Decide which child (duckling) will not return in the order of poem. Teacher reads poem as five ducklings swim across pond. Teacher can demonstrate how ducklings waddle, and how hands can be used for ducks' beak. This poem leads well into discussions about loud and soft, or "inside and outside" voices.

THE BIG, BIG TURNIP
(Traditional)

Pieces: Farmer   Turnip   Daughter   Cat
          Farmer's Wife   Large Piece of Ground   Dog   Mouse

A farmer once planted a turnip seed. And it grew, and it grew and it grew. The farmer saw it was time to pull the turnip out of the ground. So he took hold of it and began to pull.

He pulled and he pulled and he pulled and he pulled. But the turnip wouldn't come up.

So the farmer called to his wife who was getting dinner.

Fe, fi, fo, fum

I pulled the turnip

But it wouldn't come up.

Place farmer on board. Cover turnip so that only top is showing with ground piece, and place on board.

And the wife came running, and she took hold of the farmer, and they pulled and they pulled and they pulled and they pulled. But the turnip wouldn't come up.

Move farmer next to turnip with hands on turnip top.

So the wife called to the daughter who was feeding the chickens nearby.

Fe, fi, fo, fum
We pulled the turnip
But it wouldn't come up.

And the daughter came running. The daughter took hold of the wife. The wife took hold of the farmer. The farmer took hold of the turnip. And they pulled and they pulled and they pulled and they pulled. But the turnip wouldn't come up.

Place daughter behind farmer's wife.

So the daughter called to the dog who was chewing a bone.

Fe, fi, fo, fum
We pulled the turnip
But it wouldn't come up.

And the dog came running. The dog took hold of the daughter. The daughter took hold of the wife. The wife took hold of the farmer. And the farmer took hold of the turnip. And they pulled and they pulled and they pulled. But the turnip wouldn't come up.

Place dog behind daughter.

The dog called to the cat who was chasing her tail.
Fe, fi, fo, fum
We pulled the turnip
But it wouldn't come up.

And the cat came running. The cat took hold of the dog. The dog took hold of the daughter. The daughter took hold of the wife. The wife took hold of the farmer. The farmer took hold of the turnip. And they pulled and they pulled and they pulled. But the turnip wouldn't come up.

Place cat behind dog.

So the cat called the mouse who was nibbling spinach nearby.

Fe, fi, fo, fum
We pulled the turnip
But it wouldn't come up.
And the mouse came running.

"That little mouse can't help," said the dog. "He's too little." "Phooey," squeaked the mouse. "I could pull that turnip up myself, but since you have all been pulling I'll let you help too."

So the mouse took hold of the cat. The cat took hold of the dog. The dog took hold of the daughter. The daughter took hold of the wife. The wife took hold of the farmer. The farmer took hold of the turnip. And they pulled and they pulled and they pulled. And up came the turnip.

Place mouse behind cat.

And the mouse squeaked, "I told you so!"

Remove ground.

EASTER SURPRISE

Pieces: Peter   Mrs. Hen

Peter	Mrs. Hen
Big Rabbit	Basket
Hole in the ground	6 Eggs, white on one side,
6 small chicks, blue,	and blue, red, orange,
red, yellow, green,	yellow, green, purple on
purple and orange	the other (felt glued together)

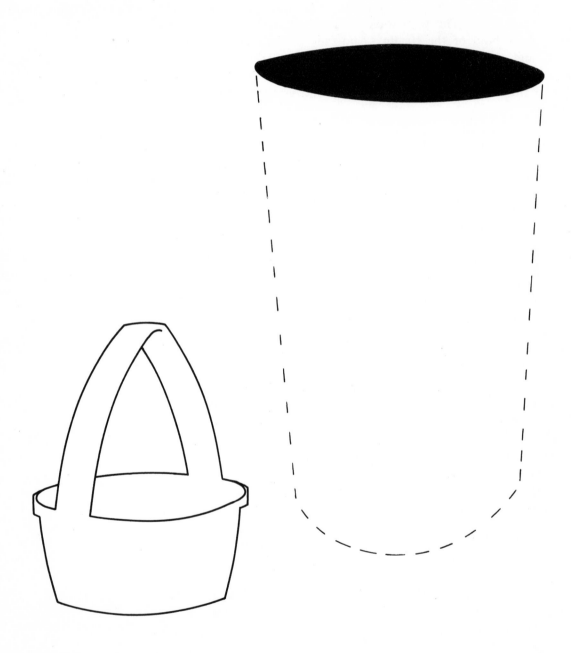

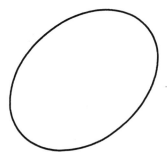

One day Peter was walking in the grass, and he heard someone crying. When he looked close he saw a big rabbit. "Why are you crying?" he said to the big rabbit. "Well," said the rabbit, "Next week is Easter and I can't find enough eggs to color!"

"I'll help you," said Peter. "That would be kind," rabbit said. "I have to hurry off now but if you find any eggs bring them to that big hole in the ground over there and stamp your foot three times.

Peter hurried off to see Mrs. Hen. "Please Mrs. Hen, I'd like to help Big Rabbit, do you have any eggs?" Mrs. Hen said, "Well I've been sitting on these eggs for a long time and none have hatched, you can have them." "Thank you," said Peter carrying them off in his basket.

"I could help Big Rabbit by coloring them too before I take them to his hole." So away he went into his house. When he came out he had an orange egg, a yellow egg, a red egg, a blue egg, a green and purple one in his basket. They looked like Easter eggs now. He hurried to Big Rabbit's hole in the ground. When he got to the hole he couldn't remember how many times he was supposed to stamp his foot, do you remember? (If a child doesn't, teacher does) "Let's all stamp our foot 3 times and see if rabbit comes out."

Big Rabbit popped up and Peter said, "Look, I've found some eggs and I've colored them." Peter lined them up in front of the basket. Big Rabbit thanked Peter and reached down to pick up the orange eggs. They heard a cracking noise. Out of the orange egg came an orange chick who said "peep-peep." They heard other peep-peeps. Out of the green egg came a green chick, out of the red egg a red one, out of the yellow egg a yellow one, out of the blue egg a blue one and then a purple one too. "You'd better take them back to

Put Peter on the board next to hole in the ground with rabbit beneath. Pull out Big Rabbit.

Place rabbit back behind hole.

Add Mrs. Hen sitting on 6 white eggs.

Add basket, put in eggs.

Take Peter and basket off board. Bring Peter back with eggs turned to colored side.

Pull rabbit up.

Take eggs out and line up.

Pull out orange chick then others.

their mother," said the Big Rabbit. Peter did, and Mrs. Hen was so happy all she could say was cluck-cluck over and over again.

Move Peter back to Mrs. Hen with chicks in basket.

    Big Rabbit did find enough eggs for all the children. Peter found a red one and a blue one in the grass on Easter morning. And Mrs. Hen was happiest of all with her beautiful Easter colored children. Cluck-Cluck, Cluck-Cluck, Happy Easter, was all she could say.

Place chicks out around Mrs. Hen.

Suggestions: Make the eggs large enough to hide chicks inside. Glue white side to colored side, leaving an opening for chick to be slipped inside. Make hole in the ground large enough to hide Big Rabbit beneath. Make basket with back side so eggs can be slipped in.

ADDITIONAL PUPPET IDEAS AND PATTERNS (UNIT 12)

PUPPET IDEAS

PAPER BAG PUPPETS

Construction: Draw a face on the upper part of bag; color. Stuff with cotton or newspaper. Put neck cylinder into head and tie string around neck. (Neck cylinder is made by rolling a piece of tag board and taping together. The roll should fit around the first finger.)

    If the puppet needs hair, paste on. Add other distinguishing characteristics. Cut hole in paper or cloth and stick neck cylinder through the hole. Paste, sew, or otherwise fasten. Add hands of paws cut from tag board.

Materials:
5" x 8" paper bag	Paste
String	Crepe paper or cloth for dress
Crayons or paint	Scissors
Newspapers or cotton	

Movement: Forefinger in neck tube.

PAPER BAG PUPPETS

Made from a paper bag approximately 6" x 11".

Construction: Paint the face on the bottom of the bag while the bag is closed and flat. The opening made by raising the bottom flap forms the mouth of the person or animal.

Materials: Paper bag, crayon, paint, or cut paper

Movement: Put hand and part of arm in bag. Put fingers over inside flap that forms the bottom. Move flap up and down to make puppet talk.

SOCK PUPPET

Construction: Use any cotton bobby sock in white, pink, yellow, light blue, tan, etc. Stuff the toe of the sock with cotton, small pieces of rags or newspaper.

Pull out a piece of the sock with the stuffing in it, and tie with a string. This makes the nose. Insert tube in neck and tie. If the sock is the wrong color, the entire face may be painted with flesh colored tempera. When dry, the face is painted on. Cut hole in cloth and stick neck cylinder through. Tie in place. Add hands and feet cut from tag board if desired.

Materials: Tag board (for hands and feet)   Cotton or other stuffing
                 Sock   String
                 Paint – Tempera   Cloth for dress

Movement: Forefinger in neck tube.

POTATO OR TENNIS BALL PUPPETS

Construction: Cut a hole the size of your forefinger in the bottom of a fairly smooth evenly shaped potato. Insert neck tube. Paint face. Add hair. It may be fastened with pins stuck into the potato. Sew dress to neck tube. Add tag board hands and feet.

Same procedure for the tennis ball.

Materials: Potato or tennis ball   Cloth for dress
                 Scissors or paring knife to cut hole Material for hair
                 Tag board

STUFFED CLOTH PUPPET

Construction: Draw head pattern and cut around it on a fold of cloth (white, tan, or pink). Sew around front and back, turn inside out, and stuff with cotton or rags. Insert neck tube and tie. Paint on face. Cut dress and sew to neck tube. Add hands and feet.

Materials: Cloth (for head and dress)   Tag board for hands and feet
                 Scissors   Material for hair (cotton, yarn, etc.)
                 Needle and thread

STUFFED PAPER PUPPET

Construction: Have the child draw himself or any character he chooses on a piece of butcher paper. Then trace and cut second figure for the back.

With needle and thread (fairly heavy – # 20) sew, with a whipping stitch, the two forms together around head, and start stuffing with cotton, paper or cloth scraps. Sew around one side, and continue to stuff until the entire body is filled. Paint entire figure with flesh-colored tempera. When dry, paint face. Add hair. Lay puppet down on cloth and measure for dress. Cut out and sew dress.

Tape stick to back.

Materials: Butcher paper   Scissors   Tempera paint   Cloth for dress
                 Needle and thread Material for stuffing Material for hair

PAPIER-MACHE PUPPETS

Construction: Wet newspaper and press into a ball, insert neck tube and tie. Add strips of newspaper dipped in wheat paste, until the entire head is covered with three or four layers. Add strips for eyebrows; push in hollows for eyes. Add a wad of paper for the nose. Fasten on with strips dipped in wheat paste. Let stand four or five days or until dry. Tear paper towels into 1" squares, dip in wheat paste and cover entire head. Let dry again. Paint with tempera. Add hair and dress.

Materials:

Wheat paste	Cloth	String
Newspaper	Material for hair	
Tempera paint	Tag board (for hands and feet and neck tube)	

IDEAS FOR PUPPET THEATRES

Fiberboard Theatre
and curtain. Use
hinges on sides so
it can be folded.

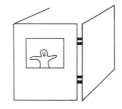

Puppet Screen
For shadow puppets.
Make by stapling old
sheet to picture frame.

Table Theatre
Use a table turned on
side. Children work
puppets from behind.

Hang a blanket from two chairs. Easy and quick.

Window
On a warm day children go outside, some stay to work puppets from open windows.

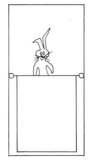

Doorway
Tape sheet across bottom half.

Refrigerator Box
Cut one side all the way down. Cut a window stage about 24" wide, add curtains and paint.

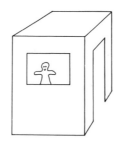

Hat Box
Tie around neck. Place hand through bottom to manipulate puppet.

Box (Cardboard)
Cut out back of
box. Place on small
table.

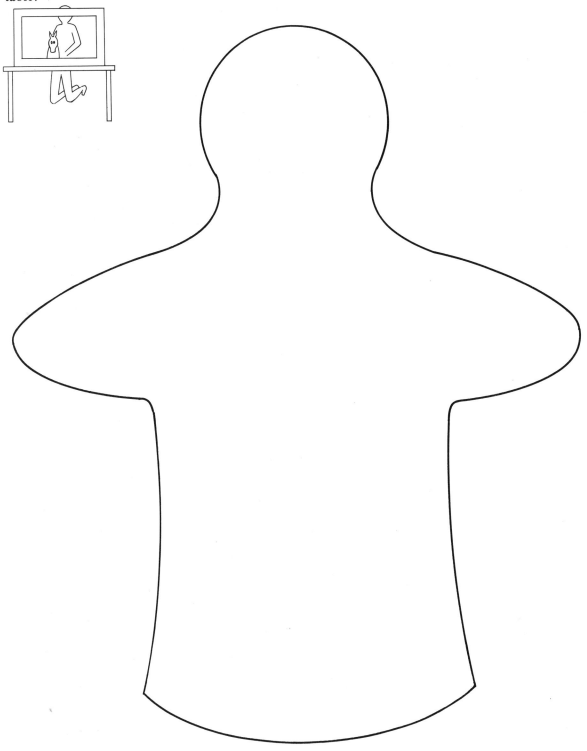

RESOURCE BOOKS FOR LISTENING ACTIVITIES

Chandler, Bessie E., *Early Learning Experiences,* The Instructor Publications, Inc., Dansville, New York 14437.

Cochran, E.V., *Teach and Reach That Child,* Peek Publications, 4067 Transport Street, Palo Alto, Calif.

Croft, Doreen J., Hess, Robert, *An Activities Handbook for Teachers of Young Children,* Boston: Houghton Mifflin Co.

Engel, Rose C., *Language Motivating Experiences for Young Children,* Educative Toys and Supplies, 6416 Van Nuys Blvd., Van Nuys, Calif. 91401.

Mayesky, M., Neuman, D., and Wlodkowski, R., *Creative Activities for Young Children,* Albany: Delmar Publishers.

Scott, Louise Binder, *Learning Time with Language Experiences for Young Children,* St. Louis: Webster Division, McGraw-Hill.

Van Allen, Roach, *Language Experiences in Early Childhood,* Encyclopedia Britannica Educational Corp.

RESOURCE BOOKS FOR PUPPETRY IDEAS

Ackley, E.F., *Marionettes: Easy to Make Fun to Use,* Philadelphia: Lippincott.

Batchelder, Marjorie, *The Puppet Theatre Handbook,* New York: Harper & Row.

Beaumont, C.W., *Puppets & the Puppet Stage,* Ann Arbor: Finch Press.

Bufano, Remo, *Remo Bufano's Book of Puppetry,* New York: MacMillan.

Ficklen, B., *Handbook of Fist Puppets,* Philadelphia: Lippincott.

Haberl, Sister Marie Anthony, *Marionettes Teach Them,* Denver: Miles and Dryer Printing Co.

Hastings, Sue and Ruthenberg, D., *How to Produce Puppet Plays,* New York: Harper.

Hoben, A.M., *Beginners' Puppet Book,* New York: Noble and Noble.

Inverarity, R.B., *A Manual of Puppetry,* Portland: Binfords & Mort.

Joseph, H.H., *A Book of Marionettes,* New York: Viking Press.

McPharlin, Paul, Editor, *Puppetry, A Yearbook of Puppets and Marionettes,* Birmingham, Michigan.

Millifan, D.F., *First Puppetry,* New York: Barnes.

Munger and Elder, *Book of Puppets,* New York: Lothrop.

Murphy, Virginia, *Puppetry, An Educational Adventure,* New York: Art Education, Inc.

Rossback, C.E., *Making Marionettes,* New York: Harcourt.

Warner, F.S., *The Ragamuffin Marionettes,* New York: Houghton.

BOOKS FOR CHILDREN

Alexander, Martha G., *Bobo's Dream,* New York: The Dial Press, Inc.

Bemelmans, Ludwig, *Madeline,* New York: Viking Press.

Borten, Helen. *Do You Hear What I Hear?* New York: Abelard-Schuman.

Borten, Helen. *Do You Know What I Know?* New York: Abelard-Schuman, Limited.

Brown, Marcia Joan. *Once a Mouse,* New York: Charles Scribner's Sons.

Craig, M. Jean. *Boxes,* New York: Grosset and Dunlap.

Eastman, Philip D. *Are You My Mother?* New York: Random House.

Flack, Marjorie. *Ask Mr. Bear,* New York: Macmillan.

Flack, Marjorie. *Angus and the Cat,* Garden City, N.Y.: Doubleday & Company.

Goudey, Alice E. *Butterfly Time,* New York: Charles Scribner's Sons.

Green, Mary McBurney. *Everybody Eats and Everybody Has A House,* New York: Young Scott Books.

Jaynes, Ruth. *Friends! Friends! Friends!,* Glendale, California: Bowmar.

Keats, Ezra Jack. *The Snowy Day,* New York: Viking Press.

Keats, Ezra Jack. *Whistle for Willie,* New York: Viking Press.

Knight, Hilary. *Where's Wallace?,* New York: Harper & Row.

Krauss, Ruth. *The Carrot Seed,* New York: Harper & Row.

Lathrop, Dorothy P. *Who Goes There?,* New York: The Macmillan Company.

Lenski, Lois. *The Little Train,* New York: Walck.

Lenski, Lois. *Policeman Small,* New York: Walck.

Lionni, Leo. *Inch by Inch,* Stamford, Conn.: Astor-Honor, Inc.

Livingston, Myra Cohn and Blegvad, Erik. *I'm Hiding,* New York: Harcourt Brace & World.

Lubell, Winifred, and Lubell, Cecil. *The Tall Grass Zoo,* Skokie, Ill.: Rand McNally,

McLeod, Emilie Warren. *One Snail & Me,* Boston: Little, Brown.

Milne, A.A. *When We Were Very Young,* New York: E.P. Dutton.

Munari, Bruno. *Bruno Munari's ABC,* Cleveland: The World Publishing Company.

Nodset, Joan L. *Who Took the Farmer's Hat?,* New York: Harper & Row.

O'Neill, Mary. *Hailstones and Halibut Bones,* New York: Doubleday and Company, Inc.

Reed, Philip. *Mother Goose and Nursery Rhymes,* New York: Atheneum.

Rey, Hans A. *Curious George Learns the Alphabet,* Boston: Houghton Mifflin Company.

Selsam, Millicent. *Terry and the Caterpillars,* Illus. By Erik Blegvad, New York: Harper & Row.

Scott, Ann Herbert. *Big Cowboy Western,* New York: Lothrop, Lee and Shepard.

Sendak, Maurice. *Where the Wild Things Are,* New York: Harper & Row.

Showers, Paul. *Find Out By Touching,* New York: Thomas Y. Crowell.

Showers, Paul. *Follow Your Nose,* New York: Thomas Y. Crowell Company.

Stevens, Carla. *Catch a Cricket,* New York: Young Scott.

Tudor, Tasha. *One is One,* New York: Rand.

Watson, Aldren. *My Garden Grows.* New York: The Viking Press.

Witte, Pat and Eve. *Who Lives Here?,* New York: Golden Press.

Williamson, Stan. *The No-Bark Dog,* Illus. by Tom O'Sullivan; Chicago: Follett.

Yashima, Taro. *Umbrella,* New York: Viking Press.

ANSWERS TO REVIEW QUESTIONS

SECTION 1 LANGUAGE DEVELOPMENT IN THE YOUNG CHILD

Unit 1 Beginnings of Communication

A. crying, cooing sounds, babbling, repeated syllables, single words, run-together words, simple sentences, compound sentences, adultlike articulation

B.
1. Heredity and environment
2. Provide experiences, love, security, warmth
3. To stimulate soundmaking; exercise vocal chords.
4. Language involves action and reaction.
5. Ears, eyes, nose, mouth, skin
6. Perception

C. 1. b   2. c   3. b   4. b   5. a   6. a, b   7. a, b, c   8. d

D. holding, providing consistent care, talking to, responding to sounds the infant makes, touching, providing social situations, providing stimuli, being warm and loving

E.
1. d   3. g   5. h   7. i   9. b
2. a   4. f   6. e   8. j   10. c

Unit 2 Characteristics of Preschool Language

A.

Age 2-3	Age 4-5
telegram sentences	75% perfect articulation
repetitions	"Look, I'm jumping"
substitutions	name-calling and swearing
omissions of letter sounds	adultlike speech
nonverbal communication	2,000-2,500 word vocabulary
talking about what one's doing	role playing
stuttering	planning play with others
talking through an adult	rhyming and nonsense words

B.

1. Debbie	Mary
Telegram sentences	Repetition
Substitution *d* for *t*	Verb tense error
Substitution *ch* for *s*	Command
Commands	Omission of letter sounds
Omission-beginning sounds	Improvised word
Repetition	Asking for recognition of an accomplishment
Omission-ending sounds	Substitution of letter sounds
Run-together word	
Pronoun errors	
Nonverbal communication	
Egocentric Speech	

    2.   Debbie

C.
1. a   3. b, c, d   5. a, b, c   7. a, b, c   9. b
2. a, b, d   4. a, b, c   6. a, b, d   8. a, b, c, d   10. a, b, c, d

Unit 3 Teaching Language

A. Modeling speech behavior and attitudes; providing opportunities for language growth; and interacting with the children.

B.

Models	Provides	Interacts
speech	opportunities	focusing attention
intonation	activities	asking questions
pitch	equipment	motivating
articulation	materials	planning repetitions
attitudes	words	giving feedback
actions	information	reinforcing
grammar	the necessity to speak	taking advantage of
sentence patterns	group situations	unplanned events
Standard English	listening	listening
courtesy words		
listening		
pronunciation		
enthusiasm		
care and concern		
problem solving		

C.

Appropriate	Inappropriate
Attempts to focus attention on the activity	Negative reinforcement of child's desire to speak
Use of please	Deny child's perceptions
Full sentences	Not answering
Clear concise speech	Not listening
Use of Standard English	Fails to ask clarifying questions
	Fails to supply words
	Doesn't pursue conversation about child's interest
	Makes speaking a task instead of a pleasure
	Omits any positive reinforcement of child's speaking

D. The child's developmental level and his individual needs.

E. 1. a and b   2. a and b   3. a, b, c, d   4. a, b, d   5. a, c   6. a, b, and c

SECTION 2 LISTENING – A LANGUAGE ART

Unit 4 Listening Skills

A. 1. Creative listening   3. Appreciative listening   5. Purposeful listening
2. Critical listening   4. Discriminative listening

B. Sustaining attention span
Following directions or commands
Imitating listening to details
Identifying and associating sounds

Discriminating by tempo, pitch or intensity between sounds
Using auditory memory

C. 1. b, d
2. b, c
3. a, b, c, d
4. a, b
5. a, b, c

6. Learning may occur in a variety of ways.
7. Intensity – an extreme degree of strength, force or energy
Pitch – the highness or lowness of sound
Tempo – the rate of speed of a musical piece or passage

Unit 5 Listening Activities

1. They move the child to listen for a signal, listen to directions, listen for sounds, perform body movements.
2. Criteria: Is the subject matter appropriate? Is it clearly presented? Is it interesting to the young child? Does it meet the teaching objective?

Unit 6 Reading Books to Children

1. b, c, l, o, p
2. a. It may be inappropriate for young children. Teacher should be familiar with it so she can present it enthusiastically. She is better prepared for discussions which promote goals.
    b. Model this behavior with statements and actions.
    c. They can make the experience successful in light of the reading goals.
3.
1. e	3. a	5. c	7. f	9. j	11. 1
2. g	4. b	6. d	8. h	10. i	12. k

Unit 7 Storytelling

A. 1. f   2. c   3. a   4. b   5. e   6. d

B. 1. a. It involves close personal contact between teachers and children while using language.
        b. It promotes childrens' storytelling.
        c. Teachers model speech usage and gestures.
        d. It is one way teachers can share their own experiences and attitudes with children.
        e. Children can create their own mental pictures as stories are told.
        f. School or life problems can be dealt with in storytelling experiences.
        g. New vocabulary can be introduced.
        h. Listening is promoted.
    2. a. Sharing problems.
        b. Physical aggression problems.
        c. Adjusting to a new baby at home.
        d. Fears of animals, bodily harm, or of the dark, etc.
        e. Almost every type of social or emotional problem in the lives of young children.
    3. a. include brief, simple definitions during the storytelling.
        b. repeat the new words and facts, and provide firsthand experiences when possible.
        c. purposefully include them, and stressing them in the context of the story.
    4. Books, children's magazines, movies, other teachers, stories created by themselves.

C. 1. a, b, c, d   2. a, d   3. a, b, c   4. b, d   5. a, b, c, d

Unit 8 Poetry With Young Children

A. 1. Promotes language development.
    2. Children enjoy poetry's rhythm, fast action, and imaginative aspects.
    3. Children can learn new words and concepts.
    4. It's easy to learn and remember for many children, therefore, it builds children's self-confidence.
    5. It's a language arts form that promotes children's speaking.
    6. Many poems add humor to the language arts program.

B.
1. j	3. c	5. d	7. g	9. h	11. m	13. o	15. 1
2. e	4. f	6. b	8. i	10. k	12. n	14. a	

Unit 9 Visual-Activities

1. Flannel, felt, or any fuzzy-textured yardage to which pieces will stick.
2. Pellon, felt, flannel, paper with any backing that sticks, such as sandpaper or fuzzy velour paper.
3. (This is a personal evaluation statement, any answer is acceptable.)
4. Focuses attention. Adds a visual representation for words used during activities.
5. c, e, d, b, e, g, f, j, a, h, i

SECTION 3 SPEAKING – A LANGUAGE ART

Unit 10 Realizing Goals

A.
1. Activities which teachers have planned and prepared during which they actively lead and direct the participation.
2. Without drawing undue attention or producing a sharp impression; "matter-of-factly," or with sensitivity. (The word was used to describe how teachers should immediately supply good Standard English form following a child's incorrect usage.)
3. Words that show ownership.
4. Words implying a denial or refusal; saying "no"
5. A relational word that connects a noun, pronoun or noun phrase to another part of a sentence such as *in, by, for, with, to*
6. A word that compares one thing with something else, or examines in order to observe or discover similarities or differences. Examples: *more, less, equal, big, bigger, biggest.*

B.
1. planned activities, daily staff-child interaction, use of equipment and materials.
2. be interested herself and focus attention on details.
3. lighting, heating, adequate movement, space, soft textures, seating arrangements.
4. eye level

C.
1. c   2. a, b, d   3. a, c   4. a, d   5. c

D.
1. Plan many activities where children have speaking successes.
2. Listen and respond to their speaking.
3. Appreciate their communication efforts.
4. Reward their speaking with smiles and answers.
5. Don't make verbal comparisons of children's speaking abilities.

E.
1. 5   2. 4   3. 1   4. 2   5. 3   6. 6

Unit 11 A Climate and Setting For Speaking

A.
1. Child's play in which children act out past experiences and creatively improvise new ones.
2. To deal with and attempt to overcome problems.
3. A regular course of procedure.

B.
1. a, b, c, e, f, i, k, l, m, n

C.
1. A collection of items, clothing or other props that would stimulate children activity and play centered around one theme such as fireman, or washing clothes.
2. Children feeling pressured to speak. Children becoming restless and bored.

D. 2, 3, 4, 5, 8, 9

E. Policeman, Nurse, Service Station Attendant, Waiter, Secretary, any vocational or occupation theme is acceptable.

F. Bonnie, you didn't say it, you were playing with your hair ribbon.
Say it now, Bonnie.
Speak louder, Susie, we can't hear you.
Not "I'm present, Brett." Say "I'm here Mrs. Brown."
David, you must answer when I call your name!
No, Andy, say "I'm here Mrs. Brown," not "I'm here" and that's all.
I don't know what's the matter with all of you; you did it right yesterday.
We're going to stay here until we all do it right.
I can't understand what you said Dana, say it again.
No, it's not time to talk to Ronnie now; it's time to speak up.
I give up, you'll never learn.

Unit 12 Speaking Activities

A. | Imitating | Creating | Expressing |
|---|---|---|
| finger plays | child using a puppet | picture collections |
| songs | acting out plays | mystery bag |
| body action chants | child flannelboard sets | daily conversations |

B. They usually learn them easily. They involved action. Children experience a group feeling. They can exhibit a learned skill to others. Once learned they produce a feeling of security and competency. They enjoy the rhyming.

C. (3) Teacher practices finger play.
(2) Teacher knows words and actions of a finger play.
(6) Teacher presents finger play to children.
(5) Child watches.
(8) Teacher encourages children to join in actions and words.
(4) Child participates with actions only.
(1) Child knows words and actions of a finger play.
(7) Teacher evaluates the results of the finger play.

Unit 13 Understanding Differences

A. 1. By visiting the home and observing the neighborhoods and communities in which her particular children reside. Parents are valuable resources in giving teachers more insights into understanding the lives and customs of the home.
2. She accepts and values them as individuals just as they are, not "as they could be."
3. By investigating the differences which exist in grammar, speech sounds, and intonation between the two languages.
4. a. The teacher did not continue the conversation with a comment that would motivate or stimulate the child's speaking further in greater detail.
    b. The teacher was admonishing and making a moralistic evaluation of the child's behavior. A better answer could have been "It hurts when someone hits us, use your words to ask Johnny for a turn with the truck when you want to play with it."
    c. The teacher has already received three verbal responses from the child without rewarding his request. The child simply gives up, and doesn't want to play a verbal game where he must ask for things in exactly the right way.
    d. In this case the child is speaking words not sentences, to define fellow is probably offering too much. A better response would have been "Here's the yellow one, Lindy" for the child's words were spoken as a question.
    e. Teacher could have shown interest, and discussed with the child where the bug was found, how it was caught, the bug's color or other characteristics, and questions which would have promoted the child's putting his ideas into words.
    f. The child probably does not understand the question. Teacher could have tried rewording the question, "What kind of ice cream do you like?"

B. Refer to text or dictionary.

C. 1. "You are playing with the ball. Throw the ball up like this." (Demonstrate *up.*)
2. "Oh, you went to get the red crayon. What are you going to do with it?"
3. "Does it have a name?"
4. "I like chicken soup too. Do you like the chicken pieces or the noodles best?"
5. "That's right, we don't run into the street. We walk after looking both ways for cars."
6. "If you don't want to play with them, what are you going to choose to play with?"

D. a. 3 c. 3 e. 1 g. 3 i. 1 k. 3 m. 3 o. 3 q. 1 or 2 s. 2
    b. 2 d. 1 f. 1 h. 2 j. 1 l. 3 n. 2 p. 1 or 2 r. 1 or 2 t. 3

E.	1.	a, b, c	3.	b, c, d	5.	b, c, d
	2.	b, c, d	4.	b, c, d	6.	a, b, c, d

SECTION 4 WRITTEN COMMUNICATION

Unit 14 Printscript

A.	1. b, c, d	2. a, b, c	3. a, b, c, d	4. b	5. a, b, c, d
B.	1. b, a, c	2. b, c, a	3. b, c, a	4. b, a, c	5. a, b, c

C. 1. They have had access to writing tools. They have seen others writing. Parents have shown interest in alphabet letters or numbers.

2. Crayons, small manipulative toys, chalk, puzzles, string beads, any toy that involves small finger, hand, or arm muscle use.

D. 1. Correct for their geographical area, large enough for young children to see, written in a left-to-right fashion, a good model for children.

2. Children do not come to school with the same home experiences or with the same maturity as other children.

3. A child's interest, motivation, mental readiness, and past experiences with symbols.

4. Say, "Yes, that is the alphabet letter named *m.*"

5. Wait for the child's lead and plan a stimulating environment with lots of interesting things to do.

6. Say it's an alphabet letter just like *f* but it's called a *b*; and/or plan interesting activities which name *b* and involve tracing the outline of *b*.

Unit 15 Practicing Printscript

A. 1. Recognize the child's effort with positive comments.

2. Use the situation to direct them to a printed alphabet in the room where, with her help, the argument could be settled and become a learning situation for both.

3. During roll taking. Labeling possessions or objects. Making signs which fit into childrens' play situations. Writing children's names on artwork. Preparing bulletin boards or charts.

B. In accordance with local printscript of elementary schools.

C. 1. Printed Bob's name in correct form.

2. Printed Chris' name over his shoulder.

3. Asked Chris' permission to write his name on his paper.

4. Answered Bob with more interest, positive reinforcement and enthusiasm.

5. Answered Sue. Printed her name and encouraged her to trace and then write it for herself.

D.	1. c, d	2. b, d	3. a, c

E. The student's name and address in printscript.

F. 1. The teacher has noticed the child's interest in printing and alphabet letters.

2. The teacher would like the parent to have a copy of the forms the child should learn. (The printscript alphabet obtained from a local elementary school.)

3. Early child attempts are often upside down or backward but this is nothing to worry about.

4. Whether the child writes or not at this age is not very important; a child's interests change.

5. The preschool will supply activities and materials in the area of printing as long as the child has continued interest in these activities

Unit 16 Activities With Printscript

A. 1. Circles, squares, triangles, rectangles, stars, dots, moon shapes or any other commonly recognized shapes, geometric or otherwise.

2. Dictated by children and written in printscript by teachers.

3. A soft pencil, eraser, yardstick, chart paper, scissors, clear contact, felt pens, crayons, paper fasteners and book pockets.

4. It helps each child know the limits of his drawing area.

SECTION 5 READING

Unit 17 Readiness for Reading,

A. 1. The teacher should listen approvingly whether the child is really reading or has just memorized the story, or is retelling the story in his own words. A positive comment by the teacher is helpful such as, "Thank you for sharing your favorite book with me."

2. Since the child has demonstrated both his ability and interest, the teacher should plan activities to expand his beginning skill.

3. Teachers suggest that the family provide for the child's interest by borrowing library books, and spending time in reading activities with the child. It is helpful for parents to know that supplying words when the child asks and offering to read words found naturally in home environments will increase the child's beginning attempts.

B. Make every effort to interrelate, or combine activities stressing how they fit together in the communication process.

C. Reading — To understand the meaning of a symbol or group of symbols by interpreting its characters or signs

or

to utter or repeat aloud the words of written or printed matter.

Readiness — A state that allows one to proceed without hesitation, delay or difficulty.

Method — A regular, orderly, definite procedure or way of teaching.

Phonics — The use of elementary speech sounds in teaching beginners to read.

Incongruities — Lack of fitness or appropriateness, not corresponding to what is right, proper or reasonable.

D. 1. b   2. c   3. d   4. a   5. c

Unit 18 Resources for Language Development Materials,

A. 1. Almost all real objects (with the exception of those which are dangerous or too large to explore) can be used to promote firsthand exploration and language development. Pictures and drawings are also useful.

2. Most programs use visuals and materials which are both commercially manufactured and teacher made. By continually reviewing new materials, programs improve and remain interesting to the children.

3. Sturdiness, teaching goals, children's individual or group interests, the maturity level of the group or child using them.

4. Periodic checking of materials, repairing worn parts or replacing them is part of the child care assistant's responsibility.

B. 1. h   3. b   5. d   7. a   9. j
    2. f   4. c   6. e   8. g   10. i

C.   (Possible answers)

Positive	Negative
• Most have sequentially planned experiences.	• A set or kit could become the total language arts program.
• Activities are included with teacher instructions.	• Set or kit goals could differ from a particular program's goals.
• Most have been designed by experts in language development.	• The set or kit may not take into consideration the needs of individual children.
• Kits and sets include commercially made visuals and teaching materials.	• Some commercial materials may not hold up under heavy use.

D.   1. b   2. c   3. d   4. b   5. d

Text Bibliography

Cazden, Courtney B., *Child Language and Education,* New York: Holt, Rinehart and Winston, Inc., 1972.

Durkin, Dolores, *Teaching Young Children to Read,* Boston: Allyn and Bacon, Inc., 1972.

Landreth, Catherine, *Preschool Learning and Teaching,* New York: Harper and Row, 1972.

Montessori, Maria, *The Discovery of the Child,* translated by M. Joseph Costelloe, Notre Dame: Fides Publishers, 1967.

Slobin, Dan I., *Psycholinguistics,* Glenview: Scott, Foresman & Co., 1971.

Spodek, Bernard, *Teaching in the Early Years,* Englewood Cliffs: Prentice-Hall, 1972.

Todd, V.E., and Heffernan, H., *The Years Before School: Guiding Preschool Children,* New York: MacMillan, 1970.

ACKNOWLEDGMENTS

The author wishes to express her appreciation to the following individuals and agencies.

David Palmer and Ann Lane for the photographs.

The student authors from San Jose City College, AD Program in Early Childhood Education.

Busy Bee Nursery School, Santa Clara, California for figures 2-2; 2-7; 6-5 and 10-4.

James Lick Children's Center, Eastside High School District, San Jose, California, for figure 5-1.

Lowell Children's Center, San Jose Unified School District, San Jose, California.

Piedmont Hills Preschool, San Jose, California, for figure 2-3.

St. Elizabeth's Day Home, San Jose, California, for figure 7-1 and 7-2.

Sunnymont Nursery School, Cupertino, California, for figure 12-1.

John Wiley and Sons, Inc. for permission to use figures 3-2, 3-4 and 11-1, from *Psychology of the Child* by R.I. Watson and H.C. Lindgren, 1973.

The staff at Delmar Publishers

Director of Publications: Alan N. Knofla

Source Editor: Angela R. Emmi

Copy Editor: Ruth Saur

Director of Manufacturing and Production: Frederick Sharer

Production Specialists: Patti Barosi, Jean LeMorta, Lee St. Onge, Betty Michelfelder, Sharon Lynch

Illustrators: Anthony Canabush, George Dowse, Michael Kokernak Chris Carline

This edition of Early Childhood Experiences in Language Arts was classroom tested at the San Jose City College, California.

INDEX

275 (4C754)